HORACE MANN LECTURE 1969

THE HORACE MANN LECTURESHIP

To commemorate the life of Horace Mann, 1796–1859, and in recognition of his matchless services to the American Public School System, the School of Education of the University of Pittsburgh, in cooperation with the Tri-State Area School Study Council, established the Horace Mann Lectureship. The striking and varied contributions of Horace Mann must ever be kept alive and be reemphasized in each generation. It is difficult, indeed, to assess the magnitude of Mann's educational services. Turning from the profession of law, he devoted his life to the study and improvement of education. He, more than any other, can truly be called "Father of the American Public School System." His boundless energy, coupled with a brilliant and penetrating mind, focused the attention of the citizens of his era on the need for the improvement and support of public schools. His services were manifold. It shall be the purpose of these Lectures to reaffirm his faith in free schools and to call to their service all citizens of this generation. It is vital that all understand the purpose and function of a free public school system in American Democracy.

Uprooted Children

Uprooted Children

THE EARLY LIFE OF MIGRANT FARM WORKERS

Robert Coles

UNIVERSITY OF PITTSBURGH PRESS

Library of Congress Catalog Card Number 70–98270
SBN 8229–3192–3

To America's migrant children and to the students I have known and worked with and learned from at Harvard College —students like Bob Blumenthal, Bill Bryson, Dan Keatinge, and Terry Oxford—whose lives, in various ways, will help our nation become a better nation, and thereby help the cause of the children described in this book.

FOREWORD

Studies such as this one by Dr. Robert Coles tell us, if we need to be told, how miserable it still can be for hundreds of thousands of American children. The children whose voices Dr. Coles has captured are the sons and daughters of our nation's hardest working and lowest paid workers—migrant farmworkers.

The voices recorded by Dr. Coles tell us about the complete poverty and rootlessness of the most neglected of our citizens. Shamefully, this neglect takes place in the world's richest and mightiest nation: able to achieve a gross national product that approaches the astonishing and almost incomprehensible figure of one trillion dollars; able also to reach for the moon and soon the planets; able, finally, to harness the incredible energies of nature; yet all the while strangely unable to assure an even halfway reasonable life for men and women and children whose efforts mean we can eat, can enjoy a rich and varied diet, can go about our business confident that somehow, in some way, our markets and our tables will receive a steady supply of tomatoes and beans and oranges and apples and cucumbers.

Few studies tell this tragic story with the intensity of this book. For few authors have Robert Coles' experience with, and understanding of, migrant families, and few books include such perceptive and eloquent quotations of migrant workers, reflecting on their own lives and the problems they alone live with. The tragedy of the story is best described by the migrant workers Robert Coles has lived with and learned from. They above all know the conditions of their lives, and they tell of tasks and choices that bring hurt to any parent.

Throughout this study, Dr. Coles also captures the special additional hardships—physical, psychological, and emotional—that come from the constant movement of migratory laborers. He writes of these hardships and the severity of migrant poverty with a clarity that makes his study come alive.

Almost ten years ago the United States Senate

recognized that migrant farm workers and their
families have very special problems worthy of
continuing study and analysis and discussion by
a special subcommittee of the larger Senate
Committee on Labor and Public Welfare. One
of the results of the work of the Migratory
Labor Subcommittee is that we cannot blame
our failure to take corrective action by saying: "We don't know enough about the matter
to do anything." I fear that, on the contrary, all
too much is known about the way migrants live,
about the various houses they occupy, about the
wages they earn, about the rights and privileges
which in large measure they are denied, about
the important laws which one after the other
do *not* apply to them. For example, we know
that the average annual income of the migrant
farmer in 1967 was $922. Recently, after a con-
siderable struggle, some farm workers became
covered by the minimum wage law, but the
minimum is held lower for them than for other
workers—$1.30 an hour as compared to $1.60
an hour—and even then is widely ignored. Far
worse is the general vulnerability, political,
social, and economic, that migrants experience.
The most recent report of the Senate Subcom-

mittee on Migratory Labor confirms that

> "migrants have either been expressly excluded, or
> written out in actual practice, from almost all con-
> ventional citizen and worker benefits enacted by
> Federal and State law. . . . Residence requirements
> bar them from participation in the political pro-
> cess, and likewise, exclude migrants from receiving
> desperately needed help from public assistance
> programs, including welfare and food subsistence
> allowances."

As for the migrant children whose lives are
described by Dr. Coles and by the boys and girls
themselves, this study describes how they work
in the fields rather than attend school, often
enough with the tacit or explicit encouragement
of local officials; how the children live in the
most primitive of shacks—broken down cabins
that lack running water, lack a pretense of adequate sanitation, lack heat and screens and even
at times windows or electricity; and how they are
inadequately protected by child labor laws or,
for that matter, by any of the laws that protect
us and make us a civilized nation. Thousands
of these migrant children are constantly on the
go, and no one wants to pay them much attention. Let them come, we seem to say, and let

them do the harvesting that needs to be done. Let them, that is, stoop and pick alongside their parents, or sit by the fields waiting for them to finish their hard labor. Then, let them go, all of them. They are not "our people." They do not belong among "us." Rather, as a county commissioner said during recent congressional hearings in Florida, they are considered to be "federal people."

Migrant parents and children are fellow citizens of ours, yet in certain respects strangers, foreigners, even outcasts who are utterly removed from the America everyone else can more or less take for granted. They belong to nobody, even though they travel all over America to find work, which certainly exempts them from the charge of "laziness" or lack of initiative. In fact they are a stubborn, hard-working group of people, who get the smallest rewards for one of the most important tasks imaginable —a state of affairs that must puzzle their children, who see how hard their parents work and know first hand how little they get. Those children are lucky if they are born in a hospital and get the barest minimum of medical care through infancy and beyond. Those children are even lucky, we have recently been discovering, if they get enough food to eat. Hungry, malnourished, often sick, those children move from county to county and across state lines. As boys and girls they learn, as this study shows, how dangerous and unkind life can be, how little there is to anticipate, how hard it is now to break away and settle down and become that most important of things (it is easy to forget just how important)—a *resident,* which means a member of a community, a voter able to exert political leverage, a union member with job security, a person eligible for dozens of services and programs and opportunities.

The right to vote in local, state, and national elections, and the right to organize and bargain collectively for better wages and working conditions may be the keys to better lives for the long exploited migrant and seasonal farm workers. There is no substitute for the ability to demand equal justice and equal opportunity and to have the political and economic influence to get these demands satisfied.

Without this power hopes are raised and then dashed; laws are passed and then ignored or violated. For example, many domestic programs that we thought were passed for the benefit of the deprived have been so convoluted, abused, and twisted that they have become tools to hold down and paralyze the very people trying to gain those powers which we demand in our own lives.

Many migrants, then, are left totally deprived, desperate, frustrated,˙ and powerless: deprived of any political or any economic power, of any cultural identity or pride— deprived of everything that most Americans take for granted.

Someday, when it is hard to say, no American child will live the way those migrant children still do. Someday new laws, adequately enforced, will insist that every single child of this great nation must have as his birthright enough food, adequate clothing, decent shelter, and, beyond that, good schools and needed medical care. First of all, though, we will have to help thousands of children find *a* home, *a* place to live and grow up, *a* neighborhood. In other words, we will have to discourage migrancy as a way of life so that every year children like

these, uprooted children, will no longer wander
dazed and fearful and confused across our land.

I welcome the chance to connect this series
of important and unnerving psychological observations to the concrete legislative issues that
face the Congress of the United States. We who
make laws cannot forget what social ills ulti-
mately mean—the child's very real grief and
hurt. Those who do studies like this one must,
on the other hand, wonder what can possibly be
done to right the obvious, glaring wrongs of
our society. The Senate Subcommittee on
Migratory Labor has already made a number of
legislative recommendations. I can only hope
that a book like this one will add to our side the
voices of thousands of newly informed and
concerned citizens whose help is necessary if
new laws are to be enacted and enforced. But
such citizen involvement is also necessary for
another reason: if this country is to realize the
order of justice insisted upon by our Declara-
tion of Independence and our Constitution,
more of us will have to find the presence of the
kind of misery migrant children must confront
every day simply intolerable—politically, so-

cially, and morally intolerable. And we must, perhaps most importantly, see to it that migrant workers obtain the rights and the powers that most of us take for granted.

WALTER F. MONDALE
*United States Senator
from Minnesota and Chairman,
Subcommittee on Migratory
Labor of the Committee
on Labor and Public Welfare,
United States Senate*

*Washington, D.C.
July 1969*

PREFACE

I felt honored indeed when I was asked by the School of Education of the University of Pittsburgh and the Tri-State Area School Study Council (Pennsylvania, Ohio, and West Virginia) to deliver the seventeenth annual Horace Mann Lecture, and thereby join company with educators like Francis Keppel and psychologists like Allison Davis, whose work, for example in *Children of Bondage,* has helped show a generation of social scientists that one can become involved in serious, controversial social and political issues and still learn a few things and do proper, seemly studies that are allowed the twentieth-century kind of sanction that goes with the designation of "research." I read my unfortunately long and sad lecture on May 21 to an audience of school officials, teachers, students, and doctors. At the time, I explained that the lecture drew upon

many years of observation done by a child psy-
chiatrist who has lived with and worked among
migrant farm workers, white and black and
Mexican-American. The lecture drew upon
taped interviews, the drawings of children, and
the direct observations of a doctor become a
social anthropologist of sorts. I asked the audience to interpret the word "education" broadly
enough—as indeed it must be these days—to
mean the rearing of children under very stress-
ful and difficult circumstances. I also tried to
place the lecture in the context of a larger effort
I have been making for some ten years now, the
effort to understand how poor people of both
races, or persecuted people, or people living particularly difficult lives, manage to deal with the
world and themselves.

The Horace Mann Lecture, greatly expanded
to make up this book, will eventually be included in a much larger volume, which in itself
is a part of a series of volumes. The first volume of *Children of Crisis,* subtitled "A Study
of Courage and Fear," dealt with the way black
and white children came to terms with the vio-
lence in the South that accompanied school
desegregation. The second volume of *Children*

of Crisis will be subtitled "Migrants, Sharecrop-
pers, and Mountaineers," and will deal with
the ways that migrant farm children, sharecrop-
per children, and the children of the hollows
of Appalachia grow up. The third will be subtitled "The South Goes North" and will deal
with life in the ghettoes of the northern cities.
This long essay will be included in the second
volume of *Children of Crisis.*

In the second volume of *Children of Crisis,*
as in the first volume, I will explain the details
of my work—matters like the way I go about
doing what I do, whom I see and for what
length of time, and under what circumstances.
Here I can briefly say that the work which gave
rise to these observations started in 1963, and
has continued for several months of each year
to the present time. I have worked particularly
in Florida, where there are some one hundred
thousand agricultural workers, and in other
locations on the eastern seaboard, along which
these people travel, up and down, picking crops
and trying to make whatever meagre living they
can under such circumstances. I did my work
by visiting families, getting to know them, in
certain cases living with them, working with

them in the fields, where they taught me how to harvest various crops, and finally, travelling with them as they move about the country— always isolated from others. Apart from the fact that all Horace Mann lectures are published, in a sense this book has an ironic and sad justification: because they grow up as nomads, as wanderers, migrant children must learn, above all, that they are different from all other American children however poor or disowned by the rest of us. So, it is only fitting that their story be given its own special space.

One more thing: I have in the past dedicated the work I do to the people described, and I always will do so. For they have taught me so much about themselves, and about myself, too, my assumptions and preconceptions, my blindspots and worse. Since this volume came about because an American university sponsors a lectureship, and since I delivered this particular lecture in the year 1969, when universities all over America were being seriously challenged, I want to take this occasion to thank the students I have met and come to like and admire in tutorial sessions, in a course, and in a seminar I have shared with graduate students and undergradu-

ates at Harvard University. I have particularly
singled out four Harvard College students because I have learned a lot from each of them
and I very much look up to them: for their
good will toward people, their kindness and
openness as persons, their humane intelligence,
their lack of self-righteousness and moral arro-
gance, their willingness to demonstrate a persis-
tent, undramatic, unselfconscious, and uncon-
descending concern for others less fortunate,
a concern which is not used as an excuse to in-
sult and assault anyone or everyone. There is
a lot that needs to be done in America. I believe
young men like those to whom I have dedicated
this book will try to do those deeds. If they fail,
these American youths, then surely our migrants will scarcely know the difference—how
much worse can their lot possibly become?—but
the rest of us will and, rather obviously, not
only the rest of us who live near our college
campuses.

Uprooted Children

F*or nine months* the infant grows and grows in the womb, in a way grows rather ironically: the quarters are limited; at the end an x-ray shows the small but developed body quite bent over on itself and cramped; yet so very much has happened—indeed, a whole new life has come into being. For some hundreds of thousands of American children that stretch of time, those months, represent the longest rest ever to be had, the longest stay in any one place. From birth on moves and more moves take place, quick trips and drawn-out journeys. From birth on for such children, it is travel and all that goes with travel—that is, forced travel, undertaken by migrant farm workers, who roam the American land in search of crops to harvest and enough dollars to stay alive, if not to prosper, or, as I have often heard it modestly put, "to live half-right."

How, in fact, do such children live, the boys

and girls who are born to migrant farmers?
What do they gradually and eventually learn;
and what do they have to teach us, the home
owners and apartment dwellers, the residents of
villages and towns and cities and states? To begin with, many migrant children are not born
in hospitals, not delivered by physicians or even
carefully trained midwives, like those who work
with the Frontier Nursing Service in eastern
Kentucky. Again and again the migrant mother
will casually describe the work she does in the
field all during her pregnancy, the travel she
undertakes during that same period of time,
and finally the delivery itself: done in the rural
cabin, or yes, done "on the road" or even in the
fields. However indifferent one may be to the
cause of such people, it is hard to accept the
fact that in the second half of the twentieth cen-
tury, in the United States of America, women
bear their children on the side of a road or in
a one room house that lacks running water
and electricity, in either case attended by a
friend or neighbor or relative, who is able to
offer affection and sympathy but not medical
help. Here is how a rather conservative grower
both confirms the existence of and objects to a

state of affairs: "Sure, some of them have their babies away from hospitals. I know that. We'd never turn them away from a hospital, here or anyplace. But they have their own life, you know, and they don't do things the way we do. It's ignorance, and it's superstition. A lot of them, they don't know where the hospital is, and they don't want to go there; and some of them, they just want to be with their mother or their aunt, or someone, and they'll scream out there. I've even heard them a couple of times by the side of my fields, and the best thing you can do is leave them alone. Once one of my men went over and tried to take them to the hospital, but they screamed even louder, and he thought they believed he was going to arrest them or something. It's awful, how ignorant people can be."

Yes, people can be very ignorant. One migrant woman I have come to know is a mother of four children. She attended school for three, maybe four, years, and then only "now and then." She admits to knowing very little about any number of things, though she does claim a certain kind of awareness of herself: "Yes sir, I've always had my mother with me, come the time to have the child, except for once, and then my sister, she was real good with me, yes sir. I has them real easy, and it's bad for a little while, but then something happens and the next thing you know the baby is crying. I bleeds for a week, and I have to keep washing myself, but soon you're not doing so bad, no sir, you're not. The first time and the second time my momma tried to take me to the hospital, you know. She comes from Sylvester, Georgia, yes sir, and she never went to any hospital herself to have us; but she said I deserved better, and she tried. She just told me when the pains started that I had to come with her, and we went to the hospital, and I got scared, but I went in, and I was shaking real bad, not because of the baby, but I thought they'd arrest us, and I'd end up having the child, my first one, in a jail.

"When we asked to see a doctor and I said I was hurting, and there'd be a baby soon, the way it looked, the nurse said who was my doctor, and my momma she said there wasn't any. Then the nurse said that was too bad, and did we have a deposit for a bed, and it was a lot, more than we ever see, and we said no, but we'd try to pay any bills we ran up and as fast as possible. Then she shook her head, and she said it was too bad, but we should hurry on up to the other side of the county, to the county hospital, and that was where we might get in, though she wasn't sure. But her hospital, it was an all-private one, and you couldn't come there except if a doctor brought you in, or if there was the money, and only then could she call up a doctor and ask him if he could come over and take the case.

"So that's what happened, and we went back, and it was good that I had my girl real easylike, my momma said. The next time we tried another hospital, but it was the same thing. So, after that, we knew what to expect, yes sir. You get to know about things after a while."

She had learned something, learned a lot actually. Ignorant, barely able to write her name, never a reader, without a diploma of any kind, even one from a secondary or elementary school, she yet had figured out how certain private hospitals are run, what "criteria" they demand before a potential patient, however much in pain and in serious medical difficulty, becomes an actual patient. She needed no teacher, no social scientist to tell her the economic and political facts of life, of *her* life.

I was gently reprimanded when I asked her whether she might not have been helped by a policeman or a fireman, who traditionally (so I thought from my work as a doctor in northern cities) respond to the pleas of women about to deliver babies: "You couldn't be *too* serious, I don't believe. Because you must know, you must, that if we ever go near the police, or the fire-people, or like that, the sheriff, then it's like asking for trouble, and a lot, too. Because they'll tell you, if you pick the crops, they'll tell you to stay away; and if you go asking them for anything, then it won't be but a few seconds and they'll have you locked up, oh, will they."

She has never been locked up, nor does she believe in keeping her children locked up, watched over, carefully controlled, trained to do all sorts of things. "I lets them be," she says when asked how she spends her day with them. In point of fact, like all mothers, she constantly makes choices, or has no choice but to make a particular choice. For instance, I have watched her and other migrant mothers begin to breast-feed their children as a matter of course. For some months I assumed they naturally *had* to do so because bottled milk is expensive, and cer-

tainly there are no physicians around to pre-
scribe this formula and that one and all the
rest of the things American mothers of the
middle class come to take for granted. Finally,
I began to notice how much she enjoyed suck-
ling her child, how long she went on doing it,
and how sad, very sad she became when at a year
and a half or so the time came to stop (for
what reason, even then? I began to ask myself).
So I went ahead one day and made an observation: "If you had a lot of money and could buy
a lot of milk at the store, would you want to feed
your small babies that way, with the bottle?"

She knew exactly what I was getting at, knew
it in a sure, self-confident way that did not have
to reduce itself into a barrage of nervous, anxious, wordy statements and counterquestions
and explanations: "Yes sir, I knows what you
means. There are times when I finds myself
wondering if I'll ever get a chance to try one
of those bottles out. I'd like to, but you have
to keep going to the store then for the milk,
and then I'd run dry—and what if I started
with the bottle and I couldn't buy any more
milk, because there was no crops, you know, and
then I'd be dry, and the baby would be suffering

real bad, she would. If I had all that money,
like you say, I'd try it, though. But I don't think
I'd want to keep away from my baby all the
time like that, and so I don't think I'd try it for
so long that I'd run dry, no sir, because I like
being near to the baby. It's the best time you
ever has with your child, if you ask me. That's
right, it's the best time."

She holds the child firmly and fondles the
child lavishly as she feeds him. She makes no
effort to cover her breasts, not before me or her
fellow workers. Many times she has carried her
infant to the field, done picking, stopped to go
to the edge of the field, fed the child, left the
child to itself or the care of its grandmother or
older sister, and returned to the tomatoes or
beans or cucumbers. Many times, too, she has
reminded me that picking crops can be boring
and repetitive and laborious, and so made very
much more tolerable by the presence of good,
clean, cool water to drink, a good meal at lunch-
time, and, best of all, a child to feed lying
nearby. She knows that the chances are that
good water and food will not be available, but
an infant—yes, the presence of an infant is
much more likely: "To tell the truth, I do bet-

ter in the field, when I know my baby is waiting there for me, and soon I'll be able to go see
her and do what I can for her. It gives you
something to look ahead to."

She plans then. She plans her days around the
crops and around the care of her children; she
and her mother do that. Sometimes they both
pick the crops, and nearby the children play,
and indeed upon occasion the oldest child, nine
years old, helps out not only with the younger
children but with the beans or tomatoes also.
Sometimes the mother works on her knees, up
and down the planted rows, and *her* mother
stays with the children, on the edge of the farm
or back in the cabin. Sometimes, too, there is
no work to be had, and "we stays still and lets
the children do their running about."

To my eye migrant children begin a migrant
life very, very early. By and large, they are
allowed rather free rein as soon as they can
begin to crawl. Even before that they do not
usually have cribs, and often enough they lack
clothes and usually toys of any sort. Put differently, right off the migrant child learns that he
has no particular possessions of his own, no
place that is his to use for rest and sleep, no

objects that are his to look at and touch and
move about and come to recognize as familiar.
He does not find out that his feet get covered
with socks, his body with diapers and shirts and
pants. He does not find out that there is music
in the air, from mysterious boxes, nor does he
wake up to find bears and bunnies at hand to
touch and fondle. In sum, he does not get a
sense of *his* space, *his* things, or a rhythm that
is *his*. He sleeps with his mother at first, then
in a few months with his brothers and sisters.
Sometimes he sleeps on a bed, sometimes on the
floor, sometimes on the back seat of a car, or
on the floor of a truck, and sometimes on the
ground.

If the locations vary, and the company, so do
other things. Unlike middle class children, the
migrant child cannot assume that internal pains
will soon find some kind of relief, or that
external nuisances (and worse) will be quickly
done away with after a shout, a cry, a scream.
One migrant mother described her own feelings
of helplessness and eventual indifference in the
face of such circumstances: "My children, they
suffer. I know. They hurts, and I can't stop it.
I just have to pray that they'll stay alive, some-

how. They gets the colic, and I don't know what to do. One of them, he can't breathe right and his chest, it's in trouble. I can hear the noise inside when he takes his breaths. The worst thing, if you ask me, is the bites they get. It makes them unhappy, real unhappy. They itches and scratches and bleeds, and oh, it's the worst. They must want to tear all their skin off, but you can't do that. There'd still be mosquitoes and ants and rats and like that around, and they'd be after your insides then, if the skin was all gone. That's what would happen then. But I say to myself it's life, the way living is, and there's not much to do but accept what happens. Do you have a choice but to accept? That's what I'd like to ask you, yes sir. Once, when I was little, I seem to recall asking my uncle if there wasn't something you could do, but he said no, there wasn't, and to hush up. So I did. Now I have to tell my kids the same, that you don't go around complaining—you just don't."

She doesn't, and a lot of mothers like her don't; and their children don't either. The infants don't cry as much as ours do; or rather, the infants have learned not to cry. They are lovingly breast-fed, then put aside, for work or because there is travel to do or chores or whatever. The babies lie about and move about and crawl about, likely as not nude all day and all night. A piece of cloth may be put under them, "to catch their stuff," but not always, and on the outside, in the fields, usually not.

As for "their stuff," as for what we call "toilet training," migrant children on the whole never, never get to see a full-fledged bathroom. They never take a bath or a shower. Sometimes they see their parents use an outhouse; and sometimes they see them use the fields. The children are taught to leave a cabin or car or truck for those outhouses and fields, but the learning takes place relatively slowly and casually, at least to this observer's eye. What takes place rather more quickly has to do with the cabin itself and the car: at about the age of two the child learns he must respect both those places, though *not* very much else, including the immediate territory around the house—all of which can be understood by anyone who has seen the condition of some outhouses migrants are supposed to use, or the distance between the cabins migrants inhabit and those outhouses or, for that matter, a good serviceable stretch of woods.

They can be active, darting children, many migrant children; and they don't make the mistake of getting attached to a lot of places and possessions. They move around a lot, and they move together, even as they sleep together. They are not afraid to touch one another; in fact, they seek one another out, reach for one another, even seem lost without one another. They don't fight over who owns what, nor do they insist that this is theirs and that belongs to someone else. They don't try to shout one another down for the sake of their mother's attention or for any other reason. At times I have felt them as one—three or four or five or six children, brothers and sisters who feel very much joined and seem very much ready to take almost anything that might (and no doubt will) come their way. Some might say the children clutch at one another nervously. Some might say they huddle together, rather as Daumier or Käthe Kollwitz showed the poor doing. Some might say they belong to a "community," get along better than middle-class children, grow up without much of the "sibling rivalry" that plagues those more comfortable and fortunate children. Some might say they "adapt" to their lot, "cope" with the severe poverty and dis-

organization that goes with a migrant life. I
find it very hard to say *any one* such thing. At
times, I see migrant children very close together
alright, but much too quiet, much too with-
drawn from the world. At times, I see children
together but terribly alone—because they are
tired and sick, feverish and hungry, in pain but
resigned to pain. Nor does this kind of observation go unnoticed by their mothers, those weary,
uneducated, unsophisticated women, who have
trouble with words and grammar, who are shy
for long minutes, then fearfully talkative, then
outspoken beyond, at times, the outsider's ca-
pacity to do much but listen in confusion and
sympathy and anger: "It's hard with the children, because I have to work, and so does my
husband, because when the crops are there, you
try to make the money you can. So I gets them
to be good to one another, and watch out for
each other. But a lot of the time, they're not
feeling good. I know. They're just run down,
the way you get, you know. They don't feel
very good. There'll be a pain and something
bothering them, and they all look after each
other, yes they do. But it's hard, especially when
they all goes and gets sick at the same time, and
that happens a lot, I'll admit.

"I guess I could be better for them, if I had more to give them, more food and like that, and if I could be a better mother to them, I guess it is. But I try my best, and there's all we have to do, with the crops to work on, and we have to keep on the move, from place to place it is, you know, and there's never much left over, I'll say that, neither money nor food nor anything else. So you have to say to yourself that the little ones will take care of themselves. It's not just you; it's them, and they can be there, to wait on one another. But I'll admit, I don't believe it's the right thing, for them to be waiting on one another so much that—well, there will be sometimes when I tell their father that they're already grown up, the kids, and it's too bad they have to worry so much for each other, because that's hard on a girl of seven or eight, worrying after the little ones, and each of them looking after the smaller one. Sometimes I think it would be better if we didn't have to keep moving, but it's what we've been doing all these years, and it's the only thing we know, and it's better than starving to death, I tell myself. So I hope and pray my kids won't have to do the same. I tell them that, and I hope they're listening!"

She tells her children a lot, as a matter of fact. She does not spoil them, let them get their way, indulge them, allow them to boss her around and get fresh with her and become loudmouthed and noisy and full of themselves. She can be very stern and very insistent with them. She doesn't really speak to them very much, explain this and that to them, go into details, offer reasons, appeal to all sorts of ideas and ideals and convictions. She doesn't coax them or persuade them or argue them down. She doesn't beat them up either or threaten to do so. It is hard to *say* what she does, because words are shunned by her and anyway don't quite convey her sad, silent willfulness, a mixture of self-command and self-restraint; and it is hard to *describe* what she does, because whatever happens manages to happen swiftly and abruptly and without a lot of gestures and movements and steps and counter-steps. There will be a word like "here" or "there" or "okay" or "now" or "it's time," and there will be an arm raised, a finger pointed, and most of all a look, a fierce look or a summoning look or a steady, knowing look—and the children stir and move and do. They come over and eat what there is to eat. They get ready to leave for the fields. They get ready to come home. They prepare to leave for yet another county, town, cabin, series of fields. They may be sad or afraid. They may be annoyed or angry. They may be troubled. They may be feeling good, very good, glad to be leaving or arriving. Whatever the mood and occasion, they have learned to take their cues from their mother, and one another, and hurry on. I suppose I am saying that they tend to be rather obedient—out of fear, out of hunger, out of love; it is hard to separate all the reasons for their obedience, or, for that matter, the reasons we learn to be compliant. I hear from the owners of farms and the foremen who manage them that migrant children are "a pretty good bunch." If the people who employ migrants by the thousands find them "lazy" or "careless" or "shiftless" or "irresponsible" or "ignorant" or "animal-like," then how can their children manage so well, even earn a bit of praise and respect here and there? "I know what you mean," the owner of a very large farm in central Florida says in initial response to the essence of that question. Then he pauses for a

minute and struggles with the irony and finally
seems to have his answer to it, which is a very
good half-question indeed: "Well, I don't know,
you take children anywhere, and they're not
what their parents are, are they?" Then he am-
plifies: "Sometimes they're better than their
parents and sometimes they're worse. You'll
find good parents and bad kids and vice versa.
As for these migrants, if you ask me, it's the
parents who have never amounted to much
and maybe they try to do better with their
kids, though they're certainly not very ambitious, those parents, so I don't think they push
their kids to be successful, the way we might.
Maybe it's just they're good and strict with their
kids, and if that's the way they treat them, then
the kids learn to behave. Of course, they can't
really spoil their kids, I'll admit. They don't
have much to spoil them with; and what they
have, they tend to be wasteful about, you know."

Life is, as the man said, lean and bare for
migrant farm workers, and their children find
that out rather quickly. Hunger pangs don't
always become appeased, however loud and
long the child cries. Pain persists; injuries go
unattended. The heat does not get cooled down

by air conditioners or even fans, and cold air is not warmed by radiators. Always there is the next town, the next county, the next state, and at every stop those cabins—almost windowless, unadorned and undecorated, full of cracks, nearly empty, there as the merest of shelters, there to be left all too soon, something that both parents and children know.

How does such knowledge come alive, that is, get turned into the ways parents treat children, and children act, behave, think, get along, grow up? How consciously does a migrant mother transmit her fears to her children, or her weariness, or her sense of exhaustion and defeat, or her raging disappointment that life somehow cannot be better—for her and for the children who confront her every day with requests, questions, demands, or perhaps only their forlorn and all too hushed and restrained presence? I have watched these mothers "interact" with their children, "rear" them, demonstrate this or that "attitude" toward them or "pattern of behavior." Always I have wondered what is *really* going on, what assumptions (not explicitly defined and perhaps not known, but there nonetheless) work their way continually into

acts, deeds, and yes, for all the migrants'
lack of education, into their words—some surprisingly and embarrassingly eloquent, to the
point that what is revealed has to do not only
with their assumptions, but mine, too. For instance, I had known a migrant farm worker, a
mother of seven children, a black, southern
lady from Arkansas two years before I finally
asked her what she hopes for her children as
she brings them up. She smiled, appeared not
at all brought up short or puzzled or annoyed.
She did hesitate for a few seconds, then began
to talk as she glanced at the hot plate in the
cabin: "Well, I hope each one of them, my
three girls and four boys, each one of them has
a hot plate like that one over there, and some
food to put on it, and I mean everyday. I'd like
them to know that wherever they go, there'll
be food and the hot plate to cook it. When I
was their age, there wasn't those hot plates, and
most of the places, they didn't have electricity
in them, no sir. We'd travel from one place
to the next, picking, taking in the crops, and
there'd be a cabin—a lot of times they'd make
the chicken-coops bigger to hold us—and the
bossman, he'd give you your food, and charge
you so much for it that you'd be lucky if you

didn't owe him money after a day's work. There'd be hash and hash, and the potatoes, and bread, and I guess that's all, except for the soda pop. There'd be nothing to start the day with, but around the middle they'd come to give you something and at the end, too. A lot of the time we'd get sick from what they'd bring, but you had to keep on picking away or they'd stop feeding you altogether, and then you'd starve to death, and my daddy, he'd say that it's better to eat bad food than no food at all, yes sir. Now no one can deny that, I do believe.

"But now it's changed for the better, the last ten years, I guess, it has. They've put the electricity into some of the cabins—no, not all, but a lot—and they've stopped giving you the food, in return for the deductions. You can get a meal ticket, and keep on eating that way, and they'll give you a sandwich and pop for lunch for a dollar or more, sometimes two, but there's no obligation, and if you save up the money you can get a hot plate and cook your own, and carry the plate up North and back down here and all over the state of Florida, yes sir. And it's better for the children, I think, my cooking. It's much, much better.

"Now, I'd like them to amount to something,

my children. I don't know what, but something
that would help them to settle down and stop
the moving, stop it for good. It's hard, though.
They gets used to it, and when I tell them they
should one day plan to stop, and find work
someplace, in a city or someplace like that—
well, then, they'll say that they like the trips we
take to here and there and everywhere, and why
can't they deep going, like we do. So, I try to
tell them that I don't mean they should leave
me, and I should leave them, but that maybe
one day, when they're real big, and I'm too old
to get down on my knees and pick those beans,
maybe one day they'll be able to stop, stop and
never start again—oh, would that be good for
all of us, a home we'd never, never leave!

"You know, when they're real small, it's hard,
because as soon as they start talking, they'll
want to know why we have to go, and why can't
we stay, and why, why, why. *Then* they'd be
happy if I didn't get them in the car to move
on. But later, I'd say by the time they're maybe
five or six, like that, they've got the bug in
them; they've got used to moving on, and you
can't tell them no, that someday if God is good
to us, we'll be able to stop and stay stopped for

good. You see, I do believe that a child can get in the travelling habit, and he'll never stop himself and try to get out of it. That's what worries me, I'll admit. I'll hear my oldest one, he's eleven, talk, and he says he thinks he can pick a lot faster than me or anyone else, and he'll one day go farther North than we do, and he'll make more money out of it, and I think to myself that there's nothing I can do but let him do it, and hope one of us, one of the girls maybe, if she meets a good man, will find a home, a real home, and live in it and never leave it.

"We tried three times, you know. My husband and me, we tried to stay there in Arkansas and work on his place, the bossman's, and we couldn't, because he said we were to stay if we liked, but he couldn't pay us nothing from now on, because of the machinery he'd bought himself. Then we tried Little Rock, and there wasn't a job you could find, and people said go North, but my sister went to Chicago and died there, a year after she came. They said she had bad blood and her lungs were all no good, and maybe it was the city that killed her, my Uncle James said. So, we decided we'd just stay away from there, the city, and then the man came through, from one of the big farms down here, and he said we could make money, big money, if we just went along with him and went down to Florida and worked on the crops, just the way we always did, and that seemed like a good idea, so we did. And with the kids, one after the other, and with needing to have someplace to stay and some food and money, we've been moving along ever since, and it's been a lot of moving, I'll say that, and I wish one day we'd find there was nothing for us to do but stop, except that if we did, there might not be much food for that hot plate, that's what worries me, and I'll tell you—it's what my boy will say and my girl—they tell me that if we didn't keep on picking the crops, well then we'd have nothing to eat, and that wouldn't be worth it, sitting around and going hungry all the time. And I agree with them on that.

"So, we keep going, yes sir, we do. I try to keep everyone in good shape, the best I can. I tell them that it'll be nice, where we're going to, and there will be a lot to see on the road, and there's no telling what kind of harvest there will be, but we might make a lot of money if there's a real good one. I don't believe I should hold out those promises, though, because they believe you, the kids, I know that now, but it just makes them good, happy childen, moving along with you, and helping you with the crops. They do a lot, and I'd rather they could be working at something else, later, like I said before, but I doubt they will."

Her children, like others I have seen and like those already described, are in a sense like wanderers from the very start. They are allowed to roam cabins, roam fields, roam along the side of roads, into thickets and bushes and trees. They follow one another around, even as their parents follow the crops, follow the sun, follow the roads which lead to yet another stop, and another and another. Nor does all that go unnoticed, except by the likes of me: "I lets them have the run of the place, because we'll soon be gone, and they might as well have all the fun they can. They want to go with us and help us with the picking, and they do sometimes, and they learn how to pick themselves, and that's what they say they'll be doing when they get big and grown up, and one will say I'll cut the most celery, and one will say I'll pick more beans than you, and one will

say tomatoes are for me, and soon they've got
all the crops divided up for themselves, and
my husband and me, we say that if the life was
better then we wouldn't mind. But you know
it's a real hard life, going on the road, and we
don't know what to do, whether to tell them, the
kids, that it's a bad time they have in store for
themselves—and you don't have the heart to do
that, say that—or tell them to go ahead and
plan on the picking, the harvesting, and tell
them it'll be good, just like you kids think. Except that my husband and I, we know it's just
not true that it's good. So there it is, we're not
telling them the truth, that's a fact."

She does tell them the truth, of course. She
tells them that life is hard, unpredictable, un-
certain, never to be taken for granted, and, in
fact, rather dangerous. She tells them whom to
fear: policemen, firemen, sheriffs, people who
wear business shirts, people who are called
owners or bossmen or foremen or managers. She
tells them that no, the rest rooms in the gas sta-
tions are not to be used, better the fields or the
woods. She tells them to watch out, watch out
for just about anyone who is not a picker, a
harvester, a farmhand, a migrant worker. She

tells them why they can't stop here, or go there, or enter this place or try that one's food. She tells them why sometimes, when they are driving North with others in other cars, the state police meet them at the state line and warn them to move, move fast, move without stopping, move on side roads, move preferably by night. She tells them that no, there aren't any second helpings; no, we don't dress the way those people do, walking on that sidewalk; no, we can't live in a house like that; no, we can't live in any one house, period; no, we can't stay, however nice it is here, however much you want to stay, however much it would help everyone if we did; and no, there isn't much we can do, to stop the pain, or make things more comfortable or give life a little softness, a little excitement, a little humor and richness.

Still, the children find that excitement or humor, if not the softness and richness; to the surprise of their parents they make do, they improvise, they make the best of a bad lot and do things—with sticks and stones, with cattails, with leaves, with a few of the vegetables their parents pick, with mud and sand and wild flowers. They build the only world they can, not

with blocks and wagons and cars and balloons
and railroad tracks, but with the earth, the
earth whose products their parents harvest, the
earth whose products become, for those particular children, toys, weapons, things of a moment's joy. "They have their good times, I know
that," says a mother, "and sometimes I say to
myself that if only it could last forever; but it
can't, I know. Soon they'll be on their knees like
me, and it won't be fun no more, no it won't."

The "soon" that she mentioned is not figured
out in years, months or weeks. In fact, migrant
children learn to live by the sun and the moon,
by day and by night, by a rhythm that has
little connection with hours and minutes and
seconds. There are no clocks around, nor calen-
dars. Today is not this day of this month, nor
do the years get mentioned. The child does not
hear that it is so-and-so time—time to do one or
another thing. Even Sundays seem to come naturally, as if from Heaven; and during the height
of the harvest season they, too, go unobserved.
As a matter of fact, the arrival of Sunday, its
recognition and its observance, can be a striking
thing to see and hear: "I never know what day
it is—what difference does it make?—but it

gets in my bones that it's Sunday. Well, to be honest, we let each other know, and there's the minister, he's the one who keeps his eye on the days, and waits until the day before Sunday, and then he'll go and let one of us know that tomorrow we should try to stop, even if it's just for a few hours, and pray and ask God to smile down on us and make it better for us, later on up there, if not down here. Then, you know, we talk to one another, and the word passes along, yes it does. I'll be pulling my haul of beans toward the end of the row, to store them, and someone will come to me and say, tomorrow is Sunday, and the Reverend, he said we should all be there first thing in the morning, and if we do, then we can be through in time to go to the fields. Now, a lot of the time there's nothing to do in the fields, and then it's a different thing, yes it is; because then we can look forward to Sunday, and know it's going to be a full day, whether in the Church, or if the minister comes here, in this camp, and we meets outside and he talks to us and we sing—and afterwards you feel better."

Does she actually forget the days, or not know them, by name or number or whatever?

No, she "kind of keeps track" and "yes, I know
if it's around Monday or Tuesday, or if it's
getting to be Saturday." She went to school, on
and off, for three or four years, and she is
proud that she knows how to sign her name,
though she hasn't done it often, and she is
ashamed to do it when anyone is watching. Yet,
for her children she wants a different kind of
education, even as she doubts that her desires
will be fulfilled: "I'd like them all, my five kids,
to learn everything there is to be learned in the
world. I'd like for them to read books and to
write as much as they can, and to count way up
to the big numbers. I'd like for them to finish
with their schooling. I tell them that the only
way they'll ever do better than us, their daddy
and me, is to get all the learning they can. But
it's hard, you know, it's very hard, because we
have to keep going along. There's always a farm
up the road that needs some picking, and right
away; and if we stay still, we'll soon have none
of us, because there won't be a thing to eat, and
we'll just go down and down until we're all
bones and no flesh—that's what my daddy used
to tell me might happen to us one day, and
that's what I have to tell my kids, too. Then,

they'll ask you why is it that the other kids, they just stay and stay and never move, and why is it that we have to move, and I don't hardly know what to say, then, so I tells them that they mustn't ask those questions, because there's no answer to them. And then the kids, they'll soon be laughing, and they'll come over and tell me that they're real glad that we keep going up the road, and to the next place, because they get to see everything in the world, and those other kids—well, they're just stuck there in the same old place."

Space, time and movement, to become conceptual, mean very special things to a migrant child, and so does food, which can never be taken for granted. Many of the children I have studied these past years, in various parts of Florida and all along the eastern seaboard, view life as a constant series of trips, undertaken rather desperately in a seemingly endless expanse of time. Those same children are both active and fearful, full of initiative and desperately forlorn, driven to a wide range of ingenious and resourceful deeds and terribly paralyzed by all sorts of things: the weakness and lethargy that go with hunger and malnutrition, and the sadness and hopelessness that I suppose can be called part of their "preschool education." Indeed, the ironies mount the more time one spends with the children, the more one sees them take care of one another, pick crops fast, go fetch water and food at the age of two or three *and* know what size coins or how many dollar bills must be brought back home, talk about the police, listen to a car engine and comment on its strengths or weaknesses, discuss the advantages and disadvantages of harvesting various crops, speak about the way property owners profit from the high rents they charge for their cabins. At the same time, of course, those same children can be observed in different moods, heard making other statements: about how tired they are, about how foolish it is to spend a week in school here and another few days there, and then a couple of weeks "up yonder," about how difficult it is to make sense of people and places and customs and attitudes, about life itself, and yes, about how human beings on this planet treat one another. One of the mothers I came to know best over a period of three years let me know exactly what her children thought and said about such matters: "They'll ask you something sometimes, and you don't know how to answer them. I scratch my head and try to figure out what to say, but I can't. Then I'll ask someone, and there's no good answer that anyone has for you. I mean, if my child looks right up at me and says he thinks we live a bad life, and he thinks just about every other child in the country is doing better than he is—I mean, has a better life— then I don't know what to say, except that we're hard-working, and we do what we can, and it's true we're not doing too well, that I admit. Then my girl, she's very smart; and she'll tell me that sometimes she'll be riding along with us, there in the backseat, and she'll see those houses we pass, and the kids playing, and she'll feel like crying, because we don't have a house to stay in, and we're always going from one place to another, and we don't live so good, compared to others. But I try to tell her that God isn't going to let everything be like it is, and someday the real poor people, they'll be a lot better off, and anyway, there's no point to feeling sorry for yourself, because you can't change things, no you can't, and all you can do is say to yourself that it's true, that we've got a long, hard row to hoe, and the Lord sometimes seems to have other, more important things to do, than look after us, but you have to keep going, or else you want to go and die by the side of the road, and someday that will happen, too, but there's no point in making it happen sooner rather than later—that's what I think, and that's what I tell my girls and my boys, yes sir, I do.

"Now, they'll come back at me, oh, do they, with first one question and then another, until I don't know what to say, and I tell them to stop. Sometimes I have to hit them, yes sir, I'll admit it. They'll be asking about why, why, why, and I don't have the answers and I'm tired out, and I figure sooner or later they'll have to stop asking and just be glad they're alive. Once I told my girl that, and then she said we *wasn't* alive and we was dead, and I thought she was trying to be funny, but she wasn't, and she started crying. Then I told her she was being foolish, and of course we're alive, and she said that all we do is move and move, and most of the time she's not sure where we're going to be, and if there'll be enough to eat. That's true, but you're still alive, I said to her, and so am I, and I'm older than you by a long time, and why don't you have faith in God, and maybe do good in your learning, in those schools, and then maybe you could get yourself a home someday, and stay in it, and you'd be a lot better off, I know it, and I wish we all of us could —I mean, could have a home."

The mother mentions schools, not *a* school, not two or three, but "*those* schools." She knows that her children have attended school, at various times, in Florida, Virginia, Delaware, New York, New Jersey and Connecticut. She may not list those states very easily or confidently, but she knows they exist, and she knows she visits them, among others, every year, and she knows that upon occasion her daughter and her sons have gone to elementary schools in those states and stayed in those schools maybe a few weeks, maybe only a few days, then moved on to another school, or to no school "for a while," even though during the period of time called "for a while" other children all over the country are at school. What happens to her children in "those schools"? What do they expect to learn when they arrive? What do they actually learn, and how long do they actually stay in school? Rather obviously, migrant children spend relatively little time in classrooms, in comparison to other American children, and learn very little while there. During the two years I worked most closely and methodically with migrant families who belong to the so-called "eastern stream" I had occasion, in the case of ten families, to check on the children's school attendance and found that each child put in, on the average, about a week and a half of school, that is, eight days, during the month. Often the children had colds, stomachaches, asthma, skin infections and anemia, and so had to stay home "to rest." Often the children lacked clothes and so had to await their turn to put on the shoes and socks and pants or dresses that were, in fact, shared by perhaps three or four children. Often the parents had no real confidence in the value of education, at least the kind they knew their children had to get, in view of the nature of the migrant life and in view, for that matter, of the demands put upon the migrant farmer who lives that kind of life. Nor did the children usually feel that what they had already learned—rather a lot if outside the schools— ought to be forsaken in favor of the values and standards and habits encouraged within schools often enough attended at best on the sufferance of the teachers and the other children.

Rather obviously migrancy makes regular school attendance, even if very much desired by a particular set of parents for their children, next to impossible. The most ambitious and articulate migrant farmer I have ever met, a black man originally from northern Louisiana, describes precisely the dilemma he must face as a parent, a worker, an American citizen: "You don't realize how hard it is, trying to make sure your kids get a little learning, just a little. I don't expect my oldest boy—he's named after me—to go on and finish school. The little schooling he'll get, it's no good, because he's been in and out of so many of them, the schools, and he gets confused, and it's no good. You'll go from one state to the next, and some times the school will remember Peter, and they'll try to pick right up with him, where he left off, and give him special teaching, so he doesn't lose all his time just finding out what's going on, and where the other kids are. But, in a lot of schools, they don't seem even to want you, your kids. They'll give you and them those sour looks when you come in, and they'll act toward you as if you're dirty—you know what I mean?—as if, well, as if you're just no good, and that's that. My boy, he sees it, just like me, even if he's only nine, he does. I try to tell him not to pay attention, but he knows, and he tries to be as quiet and good as he can, but I can see him getting upset, only hiding it, and I don't know what to say. So I just try to make the best of it, and tell him that no matter what, even if it's a little bit here and a little bit there, he's got to learn how to read and how to write and how to know what's happening, not just to himself but to everyone in the world, wherever they all are. But the boy is right clever, and he says, daddy, you're not talking the truth at all, no sir; and it don't make any difference, he says, if you get your schooling, because the people who don't want you in school and don't pay you any attention there, and only smile when you tell them you're sorry but you won't be there come next week, because you've got to move on with your family—well, those people will be everywhere, no matter where you want to go and what you want to do, so there's no getting away from them and why even try, if you know you're not going to win much."

Yet his son Peter does try, and his failure to get a decent education, an even halfway adequate one, tells us, if nothing else, that earnestness and persistence, even on the part of a rather bright child, can only go so far. Peter has always been the quietest of his parents' children, the most anxious to learn things and do things and question things. His younger brothers and sisters tend to be more active, less curious, more impulsive, less contemplative. From the very start Peter wanted to attend school and worked hard while there. His efforts caught the attention of several teachers, one in Florida and one in Virginia. He has always asked why and indeed proposed answers to his own questions—all of which can annoy his parents and apparently his teachers, too, upon occasion. I have spent an unusually long period of time with Peter, not only because he and his family have had a lot to teach me, but because sometimes the exceptional child (perhaps like the very sick patient) can demonstrate rather dramatically what others also go through or experience or endure more tamely and less ostentatiously but no less convincingly.

It so happens that I knew Peter before he

went to school, and I talked with him many times after he had spent a day "in the big room," which is what he often called his classroom when he was six or seven years old. To a boy like Peter a school building, even an old and not very attractively furnished one, is a new world—of large windows and solid floors and doors and plastered ceilings and walls with pictures on them, and especially seats that one has, that one is given, that one is supposed to own, or virtually own, for day after day, almost as a right of some sort. After his first week in the first grade Peter said this: "They told me I could sit in that chair and they said the desk, it was for me, and that every day I should come to the same place, to the chair she said was mine for as long as I'm there, in that school—that's what they say, the teachers, anyway."

So, they told him he could not only sit someplace, but he could *have* something—for himself; and they told him that the next day he would continue to have what was formerly (the previous day) had, and indeed the same would go for the next day after that, until in fact there were no more days to be spent at the school. I believe Peter's remarks indicated he was not quite sure that what he heard would actually and reliably take place. I believe Peter wondered how he could possibly find himself in possession of something and keep it day after day. Peter and I talked at great length about that school, and by bringing together his various remarks, made over many weeks, it is possible to sense a little of what school meant to him, a little of what the abstraction "life" meant (and continually means) to him: "I was pretty scared, going in there. I never saw such a big door. I was scared I couldn't open it, and then I was scared I wouldn't be able to get out, because maybe the second time it would be too hard. The teacher, she kept on pulling the things up and down over the windows—yes, a kid told me they're 'blinds,' and they have them to let the sun in and keep the sun out. A lot of the time the teacher would try to help us out. She'd want to know if anyone had anything to ask, or what we wanted to do next. But she seemed to know what she was going to do, and I'd just wait and hope she didn't catch me not knowing the answer to one of her questions. She said to me that I had to pay attention, even if I wasn't going to be there for very long, and

I said I would, and I've tried to do the best I can, and I've tried to be as good as I can. She asked me as I was leaving the other day if I would be staying long, and I said I didn't know, and she said I should ask my daddy, and he'd know, but when I did, he said he didn't know, and it all depended on the crops, and what the crewman said, because he's the one who takes us to the farms. Then I told the teacher that, and she said yes, she knew what it was like, but that I should forget I'm anywhere else while I'm in school and get the most I can learned.

"I try to remember everything she says, the teacher. She's real smart, and she dresses good, a different dress every day, I think. She told us we should watch how we wear our clothes and try to wash ourselves every day and use brushes on our teeth and eat all these different things on the chart she has. I told my momma, and she said yes, what the teacher says is correct, yes it is, but you can't always go along, because there's no time, what with work and like that, and if you haven't got the shower you can't take it, and maybe someday it will be different. I asked her if we could get some chairs, like in school, and we could carry them where we go, and they'd be better than now, because you sit on the floor where we're staying, and the teacher said a good chair helps your back grow up straight, if you know how to sit in it right. But there's not the money, my daddy said, and it's hard enough *us* moving, never mind a lot of furniture, he said. When I get big, I'll find a chair that's good, but it can fold up. The teacher said you can fold up a lot of things and just carry them with you, so there's no excuse for us not having a lot of things, even if we're moving a lot, that's what she said, and one of the kids, he said his father was a salesman and travelled all over the country—and he said, the kid, that his father had a suitcase full of things you could fold up and unfold and they were all very light and you could hold the suitcase up with one finger if you wanted, that's how light. My daddy said it wasn't the same, the travelling we do, and going around selling a lot of things. He said you could make big money that way, but you couldn't do it unless you were a big shot in the first place, and with us, it's no use but to do what you know to do, and try to get by the best you can, and that's very hard, he says.

"I like going into the school, because it's

really, really nice in there, and you can be sure
no bugs will be biting you, and the sun doesn't
make you too hot, and they have the water that's
really cold and it tastes good. They'll give you
cookies and milk, and it's a lot of fun sitting
on your chair and talking with the other kids.
One boy wanted to know why I was going soon
—I told him the other day, and he thought I
was trying to fool him, I think—and I said I
didn't know why, but I had to go because my
daddy picks the crops and we moves along, and
we have to. The boy, he thought I was trying
to be funny, that's what he said first, and then
the next time he came over he said that he'd
talked with his daddy and the daddy said that
there was a lot of us, the migrant people, and
it was true that we're in one city and out, and
on to the next, and so I had to go, it's true, if
that's what my daddy does. Then he said, the
boy said, that his daddy told him to stay clear
of me, because I might be carrying a lot of sick-
ness around, and dirt, and like that; but he said
—his name is Jimmie—he said I was okay and
he wasn't going to tell his father, but we should
be friends in the yard during the playtime, and
besides he heard his mother say it was too bad
everyone didn't have a home, and stay there

from when he's born until he's all grown-up, and then it would be better for everyone.

"I thought I might never see Jimmie again, or the school either, when we drove away, but I thought I might get to see another school, and my momma said that Jimmie wasn't the only boy in the world, and there'd be plenty like him up North, and they might even be better to us up there while we're there, though she wasn't too sure. Then I was getting ready to say we shouldn't go at all, and my daddy told me to shut up, because it's hard enough to keep going without us talking about this friend and the school and the teacher and how we want to stay; so he said if I said another word I'd soon be sorry, and I didn't. Then I forgot—we were way up there, a long way from Florida, I think —and I said something Jimmie said, and they told me I'd better watch out, so I stopped and just looked out the window, and that's when I thought it would be good, like Jimmie said his mother said, if one day we stopped and we never, never went up the road again to the next farm, and after that, the next one, until you can't remember if you're going to leave or you've just come.

"That's what my momma will say sometimes,

that she just can't remember, and she'll ask us, and we're not always a help, because we'll just be going along, and not knowing why they want to leave and then stop, because it seems they could just stop and never leave, and maybe someone could find them a job where they'd never have to leave, and maybe then I could stay in the same school and I'd make a lot of friends and I'd keep them until when I was grown-up. Then I'd have the friends and I wouldn't always be moving, because they'd help me, and that's what it means to be a friend, the teacher said, and Jimmie told me that if I'd be staying around, he'd ask his mother if I could come over, and he thought that if I came during the day, and his father wasn't home, then it would be all right, because his mother says she's in favor of helping us out, my people, Jimmie says, and she said if she had the money she'd buy houses for all of us, and she said there must be a way we could stay in one place, but Jimmie said he told her what I said: if we don't keep moving, we don't eat. That's what my daddy says, and I told Jimmie. It's alright to go to school, my daddy says, but they won't feed you in school, and they won't give you a place to sleep, so first you have to stay alive, and then comes school. Jimmie said my daddy was right, but he was making a mistake, too—because his daddy says that if you don't finish school, you'll have nothing to do and you'll starve to death, so it's best to go to school and learn whatever the teacher says, even if you don't like to."

Peter has come to know several Jimmies in his short life, and he has left several schools reluctantly, sadly, even bitterly. On the other hand, he has also been glad to leave many schools. He believes he has been ignored or scorned. He feels different from other school children and feels that one or another teacher emphasizes those differences, makes them explicit, speaks them out, and in a way makes him feel thoroughly unwanted. I knew him long enough and followed his family's travels far enough to get a fairly quick response from him after his first day in a particular school. The experience invariably would be either good or bad, or so Peter judged. He would talk about what he saw and felt and in so doing reveal himself to be, I thought, remarkably intuitive and perceptive. Yet he insisted on numerous

occasions that what he noticed other migrant
children also notice, and no less rapidly than
he. "I'm a big talker," he told me after one of
our "big talks." His younger brother, Tom,
would see the same things, though, when he
went to school; he might not put what he sees
into words, or even be fully aware of what he
senses happening, but he would know it all,
know the hurt and loneliness and isolation and
sadness, know it all in the bones, in the heart,
in the back of his mind—wherever such knowledge is stored by human beings. So Peter believed, or so I believe he believed, on the basis
of his observations and remarks and complaints
and questions, all shared with me during the
two years we conversed, in Florida and North
Carolina and Virginia and upstate New York,
each of which claims to offer children like Peter
what every American child presumably is entitled to as a birthright, a free public education: "I always am a *little* scared when I try a
new school, yes; but I try to remember that I
won't be there long, and if it's no good, I'm not
stuck there, like the kids who live there. We'll
come in and they'll tell you you're special, and
they'll do what they can to make you good, to

clean you up, they'll say, and to give you better habits, they'll say. I don't like those kinds of teachers and schools that they're in.

"Yes, I met one today. She wasn't worse than the last one, but she wasn't better, either. We could tell. She started in with what we had on, and how we could at least clean our shoes, even if they weren't good, and all that; and I said in my mind that I wish I was outside, fishing maybe, or doing anything but listening to her. Then I recalled my daddy saying it would only be two or three weeks, so I didn't get bothered, no. She asked me my name, and I told her, and she asked me where I was from, and I told her, and she asked me what I was going to school for, and I told her—that it was because I *had* to—and she smiled. (I think it was because I said what she was thinking, and she was glad, so she smiled.) I told myself later that if I'd gone and told her that I was there at school because I wanted to be a teacher, like her, or even the principal, then she'd have come after me with the ruler or the pointer she has in her hand all the time. Well, I figure we'll get a good rest there, and the chairs are good, and they give you the milk and cookies, and my momma says

that's worth the whole day, regardless of what
they say, but I think she's wrong, real wrong.

"To me a good school is one where the
teacher is friendly, and she wants to be on your
side, and she'll ask you to tell the other kids
some of the things you can do, and all you've
done—you know, about the crops, and like that.
There was one teacher like that, and I think it
was up North, in New York it was. She said that
so long as we were there in the class she was
going to ask everyone to join us, that's what she
said, and we could teach the other kids what
we know and they could do the same with us.
She showed the class where we travelled, on the
map, and I told my daddy that I never before
knew how far we went each year, and he said
he couldn't understand why I didn't know, because I did the travelling all right, with him,
and so I should know. But when you look on
the map and hear the other kids say they've
never been that far, and they wish someday
they could, then you think you've done something good, too, and they'll tell you in the recess
that they've only seen where they live and we've
been all over. I told my daddy what they said,
and he said it sure was true, that we've been all

over, and he hopes the day will come when we'll be in one place, but he sure doubts it, and if I wanted I could tell the teacher he said so—but I didn't. I don't think she'd know how to answer daddy, except to say she's sorry, and she's already told us that, yes she did, right before the whole class. She said we had a hard life, that's what, the people who do the picking of the crops, and she wanted us to know that she was on our side, and she wanted to help us learn all we could, because it would be better for us later, the more we knew, and maybe most of us would find a job and keep it, and there'd be no more people following the crops all over, from place to place, and it would be better for America, she said. Then she asked if I agreed, and I didn't say one way or the other, and she asked me to just say what I thought, and I did. I said I'd been doing enough of travelling, and I'd seen a lot of places, and I wouldn't mind stopping for a change, no ma'am, and if we just stayed there, in that town, and I could go to school there—well, that would be alright by me, and it would be better than some of the other places we stop, I could say that right off, a real lot better.

"There'll be times when I wish I'd have been born one of the other kids, yes sir; that's how I sometimes think, yes. Mostly, it's when the teacher is good to you—then you think you'd like to stay. If the teacher is bad, and the kids don't speak to you, then you want to go away and never come back, and you're glad that you won't stay there too long. Now school is good, because it's a good school and they pays attention to you; most of the time though, in other schools, you just sit there, and you want to sleep. Suddenly the teacher will ask you what you're thinking, and you tell her the truth, that you don't know. Then she'll ask you what you want to be, and I don't know what to answer, so I say I'd like to work like my daddy at the crops or maybe one day get a job in the city and stay there. Then they'll tell you to study hard, the teachers, but they don't give you much to do, and they'll keep on asking you how the crops are coming, and how long you'll be there, and when are you going to be going, and like that. Sometimes I won't go to school. I tell my momma that I'm not going and can I help take care of my brothers and can I help in the field, or anything, and she'll say yes, mostly, unless she thinks the police will be getting after me, for not being in school. But most of the time they don't care, and they'll tell you you're doing good to be caring for your brother and work- ing. Yes sir, they'll drive by and wave and they don't seem to mind if you're not in school. Once a policeman asked me if I liked school and I said sometimes I did and then he said I was wasting my time there, because you don't need a lot of reading and writing to pick the crops, and if you get too much of schooling, he said, you start getting too big for your shoes and cause a lot of trouble, and then you'll end up in jail pretty fast and never get out if you don't watch your step—never get out."

Peter seeks consolation from such a future; and he often finds it by looking back to earlier years and occasions. In his own brief life as a young child, a young migrant, a young boy of eight or nine or ten, he has begun to find that the one possession he has and cannot lose is yes- terday, the old days, the experiences that have gone but remain—and remain not only in the mind's memories and dreams but in the lives of others, those brothers or sisters who are younger and who continually present a child like Peter with himself. Everything they do reminds Peter of what he once did and indeed can continue to do as the older brother become companion of younger children. I found myself concluding and in my notes emphasizing all of that, Peter's tendency to *go back,* to flee the present for the sake of the past. After all, I had to repeat to myself again and again, Peter finds school useless or worse. He finds his parents tired and distracted or worse. He finds himself at loose ends: I am a child, yet today I can work, tomorrow I may be told I'm to attend school, the next day I'll be on the road again and unsure where I shall soon be, when I shall again be still for a while, sitting on the ground, that is, or in a cabin, rather than upon the seat of a car or a bus. In the face of such uncertainties, earlier moments and ways and feelings become things (if such is the word) to be tenaciously grasped and held. And so, Peter will help pick beans and do a very good job at moving up and down the rows, but soon thereafter he will be playing on his hands and knees with his younger brothers and sucking lollipops with them and lying under a tree and crawling about and laughing with them. His mother in her own way takes note of what happens and needs no prodding from any observer to describe the sequence of events: "I think stooping for those beans can go to your head. You get dizzy after a day of it, and you want to go down on your back and stretch yourself all you can and try to feel like yourself again, and not all curled up on yourself. If Peter goes along with his daddy and me and does the stooping and picking, then he'll be real tired at the end of the day, and it seems he wants to be like my little ones. And I say to myself if it'll help him feel any better, after all that work, then Lord he can do what he likes, and if I had it in me to keep them all little babies, then I'd do it, because that's when they're truly happiest, yes sir."

Yet it turns out that her children and thousands of other migrant children are not very happy for very long; actually, many of those children have a hard time understanding the many contradictions that plague their lives. For one thing, as already indicated, migrant children of two or three years are allowed a good deal of active, assertive freedom in some respects. They are encouraged to care for one another, but also encouraged to fend for themselves: go exploring in the woods or the fields, play games almost anywhere and anytime, feel easy and relaxed about time, about schedules, about places where things are done and about routines that give order to the doing of those things. Again and again I have seen migrant children leave their cabins for the day and return anytime, when and if they pleased, to get themselves a bottle of pop and make for themselves a meal of "luncheon meat" and bread and potato chips or, often enough, potato chips and potato salad and coke. At the same time, however, those very children are also taught obedience and a real and powerful kind of fatalism: one can only go here or do that and, most of all, must submit to all the demands and confusion and sadness of travel—always the travel, inevitably the travel, endlessly the travel, all of which can amount to a rather inert and compliant and passive life. By the same token, the child is both told the grim facts of his particular life and given dozens of stories and excuses and explanations and promises whose collective function, quite naturally and humanly, is to blunt the awful, painful edges of that very life. It can even be said that migrant children obtain and learn to live with an almost uncanny mixture of realism and mysticism. It is as if they must discover how difficult their years will be, but also acquire certain places of psychological and spiritual refuge. Naturally, each family has its own particular mixture of sentiment and hard facts to offer and emphasize, even as each child makes for himself his very own nature: he becomes a blend of the assertive and the quiet, the forceful and the subdued, the utterly realistic and the strangely fanciful. What I am saying, of course, goes for all children, but at the same time I must insist that migrant children have a very special psychological fate—and one that is unusually hard for them to endure.

For example, I mentioned earlier that migrant children tend to be close to one another, tend to care very much for one another, tend almost to absorb themselves in one another, and certainly—the first observation one like me makes when he comes to know them—tend to touch one another, constantly and reassuringly and unselfconsciously and most of the time rather tenderly. At the same time those same children, literally touching to one another, can

appear more and more untouched—indifferent,
tired, bored, listless, apathetic, and finally, most
ironically, isolated physically as well as psychologically. Many of them, unlike the boy Peter
just discussed, abandon themselves to a private
world that is very hard for any outsiders to
comprehend, even a mother or father. School
means nothing, is often forsaken completely,
even the pretense of going. Friends are an affair
of the moment, to be forsaken and lost amid
all the disorder and turmoil and instability that
goes with one move after another. Sports, or-
ganized and progressively challenging sports,
are unknown. Needless to say, the migrant child
does not go to restaurants, theatres, movies,
museums, zoos and concerts. Nor do those television sets he watches work very well; they are
old and half-broken to start with, purchased
secondhand (with a bit of luck) on a never-
ending installment basis; and, in addition, as
Peter's mother puts it, "Way out in the country
you can't pick up the pictures," particularly
when there is no antenna, and the set has been
bouncing around for miles and miles, as indeed
have its owners.

It is hard to convey such experiences, such a

world, to those who don't see it and feel it and smell it and hear it. It is even harder to describe that world as it is met and apprehended and suffered by hundreds of thousands of parents and children. I say this not as a preliminary exercise in self-congratulation—what is hard is being done and therefore deserves admiration —but to warn myself and the reader alike, particularly at this point, against the temptation of psychological categorization, the temptation to say that migrant children are this or that, are "active" or "passive," resort to excessive "denial" and too many "rationalizations" and "projections," or resort to an almost brutal kind of realism, a kind of self-confrontation so devoid of humor and guile and hope and patience as to be a caricature of the analysis the rest of us value, be it psychological or political or philosophical. Put differently, I am saying that migrant children are many things, and do many things with their brief and relatively sad lives. They can be ingenious and foolish. They can have all sorts of illusions, and they can speak about themselves with almost unbearable candor and severity and gloom. They can feel disgusted with their lot, or they can pay no

attention to it, simply endure what has to be;
or they can romp and laugh and shout, even
though their observer knows how close to the
surface are the ready tears and, too, how over-
worked even the fun seems at times, the kind
of thing, of course, that can happen to all of us.

In a sense, as I write about these young children, I am lost, and want to be. I want to emphasize how literally extraordinary and, in fact,
how extraordinarily cruel their lives are: the
constant mobility; the leave-takings and the
fearful arrivals; the demanding work even
they, let alone their parents, often manage to
do; the extreme hardship that goes with a
meagre (at best) income; the need always to
gird oneself for the next slur, the next sharp
rebuke, the next reminder that one is different
and distinctly unwanted, except, naturally, for
the work that has to be done in the fields. I
also want to emphasize that extremely hard-
pressed people can find their own painful,
heavy-hearted way, can learn to make that way
as bearable as possible and can laugh not only
because they want to cry (that, too), not only in
bitter, ironic resignation (the very kind melan-
choly philosophers allow themselves to express

with a wan smile) but because it has been possible, after all the misery and chaos—yes, it has been possible—to carve a little joy out of the world. I suppose I mean that life is peculiarly and unspeakably bad for migrant farmers, but that they are, finally—well, human. That is to say, they make do, however sullenly and desperately and wildly and innocently and shrewdly, and they teach their children unsystematically but persistently that they, too, must survive, somehow, some way, against whatever odds.

Peter's mother, over the years, has essentially told me about that, about the facts of survival, not because I asked her what she has in mind when she punishes or praises her children or tells them one or another thing, but because she constantly does things for, with, and to her children. In a moment of quiet conversation her deeds, thousands of them done over many, many years, sort themselves out and find their own pattern, their own sense, their own words—not perfect or eminently logical or completely consistent words, but words that offer vision and suggest blindness and offer confidence and suggest anxiety, words, in other terms, that qualify as the responses of a hard-working and God-fearing mother who won't quite surrender but also fears she won't quite avoid a terrible and early death: "I worry every day. It'll be a second sometime in the morning or in the afternoon or most likely before I drop off to sleep. I worry that my children will wake up one time and find I'm gone. It might be the bus will go crashing, or the car or the truck on the way to the farm, or it might be I've just been called away from this bad world by God, because He's decided I ought to have a long, long rest, yes sir. Then I'll stop and remind myself that I can't die, not just yet, because there's the children, and it's hard enough for them, yes it is—too hard, if you ask me. Sometimes I'll ask myself why it has to be so hard, and why can't we just live like other people you see from the road, near their houses, you know. But who can question the Lord, that's what I think. The way I see it, I've got to do the best I can for my children, all of them. So, I keep on telling them they've got to be good, and take care of each other, and mind me and do what I says. And I tell them I don't want them getting smart ideas, and trying to be wild and getting into any trouble, because you know—well, the way I sees the world, if you're born on the road, you'll most likely have to stay with it, and they're not going to let go of you, the crewman and the sheriff and like that, and if they did, we'd be at a loss, because you go into the city, I hear, and it's worse than anything that ever was, that's what we hear all the time.

"I'm trying to make my children into good children, that's what. I'm trying to make them believe in God and listen to Him and obey his Commandments. I'm trying to have them pay me attention, and my husband, their daddy, pay him attention, and I'd like for all of them to know what they can, and grow into good people, yes, and be a credit to their daddy and me. I knows it's going to be hard for them, real bad at times, it gets. I tell them that, and I tell them not to be too set on things, not to expect that life is going to be easy. But I tell them that every man, he's entitled to rest and quiet some of the time, and we all can pray and hope it'll get better. And I tell them it used to be we never saw any money at all, and they'd send you up in those small trucks, but now they'll pay you some, and we most often have a car—we lose it, yes sir, when there's no work for a few weeks and then we're really in trouble—and we have more clothes now than we ever before had, much more, because most of my children, they have their shoes now and clothes good enough for church, most of the time. So you can't just feel sorry about things, because if you do, then you'll just be sitting there and not doing anything—and crying, I guess. Sometimes I do; I'll wake up and I'll find my eyes are all filled up with tears, and I can't figure out why, no sir. I'll be getting up, and I'll have to wipe away my eyes, and try to stop it, so the children don't think something is wrong, and then, you know, they'll start in, too. Yes, that has happened a few times, until I tell us all to go about and do something, and stop, stop the crying right away.

"You can't spend your one and only life wishing you had another life instead of the one you've got. I tell myself that, and then the tears stop; and if the children are complaining about this or that—well, I tell them that, too. I tell them it's no use complaining, and we've got to go on, and hope the day will come when it's better for us, and maybe we'll have a place to rest, and never again have to 'go on the season' and move and keep on moving and get ourselves so tired that we start the day in with the crying. Yes, sir, I believe I cry when I'm just so tired there isn't anything else to do but cry. Or else it's because I'll be waking up and I know what's facing us—oh, I do—and it just will be too much for me to think about, so I guess I go and get upset before I even know it, and then I have to pinch myself, the way my own momma used to do, and talk to myself the way she would, and say just like her: 'There's no use but to go on, and someday we'll have our long, good rest.' Yes sir, that's what she used to say, and that's what I'll be saying on those bad mornings; and you know, I'll sometimes hear my girl telling herself the same thing, and I'll say to myself that it's good she can do it now, be-cause later on she'll find herself feeling low, and then she'll have to have a message to tell herself, or else she'll be in real bad trouble, real bad trouble."

Mothers like her possess an almost uncanny mixture of willfulness and sadness. Sometimes they seem to do their work almost in spite of themselves; yet at other times they seem to take

the sad and burdensome things of life quite in
stride. As they themselves ask, What else can
they do? The answer, of course, is that complete
disintegration can always be an alternative—
helped along by cheap wine, and the hot sun,
and the dark, damp corners of those cabins,
where one can curl up and for all practical
purposes die. Migrant mothers know all that,
know the choices they have, the possibilities
that life presents. Migrant mothers also know
what has to be done, so that the children, those
many, many children, will at least eat something, will somehow get collected and moved
and brought safely to the new place, the new
quarters, the next stop or spot or farm or camp
or field, to name a few destinations such
mothers commonly mention when they talk to
me about what keeps them in half-good spirits.
I will, that is, ask how they feel, and how they
and their children are getting along, and they
will answer me with something like this: "I'm
not too bad, no sir, I'm not. We keeps going, yes
sir, we do. If you don't keep going, you're gone,
I say. You have to keep moving and so you don't
have time to stop and get upset about things.
There's always another spot to get to, and no

sooner do you get there, well, then you have to get yourself settled. There'll be yourself to settle and there'll be the kids and their daddy, too, and right off the work will be there for you to do, in the fields and with the kids, too. So, the way I see it, a mother can't let herself be discouraged. She's got to keep herself in good spirits, so her children, they'll be doing fine; because if I'm going to get all bothered, then sure enough my kids will, and that won't be good for them or me neither, I'll tell you. That's why I never lets myself get into a bad spell."

Actually, she does indeed get into bad spells, spells of moodiness and suspicion and petulance and rage, and so do her children from time to time, particularly as they grow older and approach the end of childhood. By definition life for migrants is a matter of travel, of movement; and their children soon enough come to know that fact, which means they get to feel tentative about people and places and things. Anything around is only precariously theirs. Anything soon to come will just as soon disappear. Anything left just had to be left. As a matter of fact, life itself moves, moves fast and without those occasions or ceremonies that give the rest of us a few footholds. The many young migrant children I have observed and described to myself as agile, curious, and inventive are, by seven or eight, far too composed, restrained, stiff and sullen. They know even then exactly where they must go, exactly what they must do. They no longer like to wander in the woods or poke about near swamps. When other children are just beginning to come into their own, just beginning to explore and search and take over a little of the earth, migrant children begin to lose interest in the world outside them. They stop noticing animals or plants or trees or flowers. They don't seem to hear the world's noises. To an outside observer they might seem inward, morose, drawn and tired. Certainly some of those qualities of mind and appearance have to do with the poor food migrant children have had, with the acumulation of diseases that day after day cause migrant children pain and weakness. Yet, in addition, there is a speed, a real swiftness to migrant living that cannot be overlooked, and among migrant children particularly the whole business of growing up goes fast, surprisingly fast, awfully fast, grimly and decisively fast. At two or three, migrant children see their parents hurry, work against time, step on it, get a move on. At three or four those same children can often be impulsive, boisterous, eager, impatient in fact, and constantly ready—miraculously so, an observer like me feels—to lose no time, to make short work of what is and turn to the next task, the next ride.

However, at six or eight or ten something else has begun to happen; children formerly willing to make haste and take on things energetically, if not enthusiastically, now seem harried as they hurry, breathless and abrupt as they press on. I do not think I am becoming dramatic when I say that for a few, first feverish years migrant children are hard-pressed but still and obviously quick, animated; tenacious of life is perhaps a way to say it. Between five and ten, though, those same children experience an ebb of life, even a drain of life. They move along alright; they pick themselves up again and again, as indeed they were brought up to do, as their parents continue to do, as they will soon, all too soon, be doing with their own children. They get where they're going, and to a casual eye they

seem active enough, strenuous workers in the
field, on their toes when asked something or
called to do something. Still, their mothers
know different; their mothers know that a
change is taking place, has taken place, has to
take place; their mothers know that life is short
and brutish, that one is lucky to live and have
the privilege of becoming a parent, that on the
road the days merge terribly, that it is a matter
of rolling on, always rolling on. So they do that,
the mothers, go headlong into the days and
nights, obey the commands of the seasons and
pursue the crops; and meanwhile, somewhere
inside themselves, they make their observations
and their analyses, they take note of what happens to themselves and their children: "My little ones, they'll be spry and smart, yes they will
be; but when they're older—I guess you'd say
school age, but they're not all the time in school,
I'll have to admit—then they're different, that's
what I'd say. They'll be drowsy, or they won't be
running around much. They'll take their time
and they'll slouch, you know. They'll loaf
around and do only what they think they've got
to do. I guess, well, actually, I suppose, they're
just getting grown, that's what it is. My boy, he's

the one just nine this season; he used to be up and doing things before I even knew what he was aiming to do; but now he'll let no one push him, except if he's afraid, and even then he'll be pulling back all he can, just doing enough to get by. The crewleader, he said the boy will be 'another lazy picker' and I stood up and spoke back. I said we gets them in, the beans, don't we and what more can he want, for all he pays us? I'll ask you. I guess he wants our blood. That's what I think it is he wants, and if he sees my children trying to keep some of their blood to themselves, then he gets spiteful about them and calls them all his names like that; and there isn't anything you can do but listen and try to go on and forget."

She tries to go on and forget. So do her children, the older they get. Once wide awake, even enterprising, they slowly become dilatory, leaden, slow, laggard, and lumpish. Necessarily on the move a lot, they yet appear motionless. Put to work in the fields, they seem curiously unoccupied. The work gets done, and by them, yet they do not seem to work. I suppose I am saying that older migrant children begin to labor, to do what they must do if they are not to be without a little money, a little food; but at the same time the work is not done in a diligent, painstaking and spirited way. It is done, all that hard, demanding work; the crops get taken in. What one fails to see, however, is a sense of real purpose and conviction in the older children who, like their parents, have learned that their fate is of no real concern to others. The point is survival: mere survival at best, survival against great odds, survival that never is assured and that quite apparently exacts its costs. If I had to sum up those costs in a few words I would probably say care is lost: the child stops caring, hardens himself or herself to the coming battle, as it is gradually but definitely comprehended, and tries to hold on, persist, make it through the next trip, the next day, the next row of crops.

So, all year round, all day long, hour after hour, migrants stoop or reach for vegetables and fruit, which they pull and pick and cut; and at the same time those migrants settle into one place or prepare the move to another; and at the same time those migrants try to be parents, try stubbornly to do what has to be done—feed the children and get them to listen and respond and do this rather than that, and now rather than later. I have described the determination that goes into such a life of travel and fear and impoverishment and uncertainty. I have described the first and desperate intimacy many migrant children experience with their mothers. I have described the migrant child's developing sense of his particular world with its occasional pleasures, its severe restrictions, its constant flux, its essential sameness. To do so I have drawn upon what can actually be considered the best, the most intact, of the people I have seen and heard. After all, when parents and children together live the kind of life most migrants do, it seems a little miraculous that they even halfway escape the misery and wretchedness—that is, manage to continue and remain and last, last over the generations, last long enough to work and be observed by me or anyone else.

There is, though, the misery; and it cannot be denied its importance, because not only bodies but minds suffer out of hunger and untreated illness; and that kind of psychological suffering also needs to be documented. Nor can an observer like me allow his shame and guilt and horror and outrage and sympathy and

pity and compassion to turn exhausted, care-
worn, worried, suffering people into brave and
honorable and courageous fighters, into heroes
of sorts, who, though badly down on their luck,
nevertheless manage to win out, at least spiritu-
ally and psychologically. I fear that rather another kind of applause is in order, the kind that
celebrates the struggle that a doomed man
nevertheless at least tries to make. I fear that
migrant parents and even migrant children do
indeed become what some of their harshest and
least forgiving critics call them: listless, apathetic, hard to understand, disorderly, subject
to outbursts of self-injury and destructive vio-
lence toward others, and on and on. I fear that
it is no small thing, a disaster almost beyond
repair, when children grow up, literally, adrift
the land, when they learn as a birthright the
disorder and early sorrow that goes with virtual
peonage, with an unsettled, vagabond life. In
other words, I fear I am talking about millions
of psychological catastrophes, the nature of
which has also been spelled out to me by migrant parents and migrant children. The father
of six of those children, both a hard worker
and a beaten and sad man, can talk and talk

about his failures and his overriding sense of defeat, about his sense of ruin at the hands of a relentless and compelling fate whose judgment upon him and those near him and like him simply cannot be stayed: "There will be a time, you know, when I'll ask myself what I ever did, maybe in some other life, to deserve this kind of deal. You know what I mean? I mean I feel there must be someone who's decided you should live like this, for something wrong that's been done. I don't know. I can't say it any other way. All I know is that it's no life, trying to pick beans on fifty farms all over the country, and trying to make sure your kids don't die, one after the other. Sometimes we'll be driving along and I say to myself that there's one thing I can do to end all of this for good, and it would save not only me but the children a lot of hardship, a lot. But you can't do that; I can't, at least. So, instead I go and lose my mind. You've seen me, yes you have; and I know I'm going to do it. I start with the wine, when I'm working, just so the hours will go faster, and I won't mind bending over—the pain to my back —and I won't mind the heat. There'll be days when I work right through, and there'll be days when I stop in the middle of the day, because I don't want to get sick. But there will be other days when I hear myself saying that I've got to let go, I've just got to. I've got to get so drunk that I'm dead, dead in my mind, and then if I live after it, that's fine, and if I never wake up, that's fine, too. It's not for me to decide, you see. We can't decide on anything, being on the road, and owing everything to the crewleaders and people like that. The only thing we can decide, my daddy used to tell me, is whether we'll stay alive or whether we won't. He said no matter what, we should keep going; but he got killed when the bus that was taking him and a lot of others got stalled right on a railroad track and it was crushed into little pieces by the train. I'll think of him, you know, when I get full of wine. I'll think of him telling me that you can't figure out what's the reason the world is like it is; you can only try to keep from dying, and it may take you your entire life to do that —and I guess he didn't expect that suddenly he'd be gone, after all the work he put in just to stay alive."

His wife has some observations to make about him and the effort he makes to stay alive:

"My husband, he's a good man a lot of the time. He never talks about the children, not even to me, but he loves them, I know he does. Once he told me that it hurts him every time one of our children is born, because he knows what's ahead for them. You know something? Each time, with each child, he's gone and got worse drunk than any other time. I don't know why, just that it's happened. He almost killed me and all the children the last time. He had a knife and he said he might use it. Then he took us all in the car; he made us get in, and he said if I didn't go along with him, he'd kill me, and if I did, there was a chance I'd live, and the children, too. So, I did, and he drove with his foot pressing on the gas all the way down. I could hear him trying to go faster, pushing on the pedal and trying to force it, and thank God the floor of the car wouldn't let him have his way. Well, he cursed us all, but most of all himself. He was after himself. He was chasing himself. He kept on saying that he had to catch himself and he had to get a hold on himself, and if he didn't, then he might as well die. In between, he'd tell us we were all going to die, and the sooner the better, because the only way for us to have peace, to have rest, was to die. There was no other way, he kept on shouting that to us.

"Then I must have lost my mind, like he had lost his. I started crying, and I can remember screaming to God please to turn my husband and me and the children away from Him, because it wasn't time yet, no it wasn't, for us to see Him. Then I crawled down, I reached down, I don't remember how I did, and pulled his foot away from the gas, and he didn't try to put it back, no he didn't; and the car went on and on, and then it began to slow down, and then it stopped, and then before he had a change of mind, I got out and I got all of us out, all except him, and we didn't leave him, though. (Where could we go? I didn't know where we were, and it was dark.) We spread ourselves down nearby to the car, and we tried to rest. I looked up at the sky and I couldn't forget it for the rest of my life, what I saw then and what I thought, no sir, I couldn't. When I die I know I'll be thinking like that and I'll be seeing like that: there was the sky, and it was dark, but the moon was there, almost round, and it hung low, real low, and it was colored funny, orange I guess; and all the stars were there, all over, everywhere it seemed. I'd never looked long enough to see so many stars, even though we do a lot of travelling, and we're up through the night, and you might have thought I'd have noticed them, all the stars, before. But moving across the country, you forget about the sky, I guess. (I told my boy that, a few days later I did, that we shouldn't forget the sky, because we're going along underneath it a lot of the time, and he said that maybe we forget it because it's like a roof to us, and that if you're under a roof, you never look at it.)

"While I was staring up there at the sky, I thought I heard something, a noise. It was the wind, I know, but to me it was God; it was God as well as the wind, and He was there, speaking right into both my ears, telling me to stay where I was, with the children, and near my husband, and He was looking over us, yes, and He'd see that the day would come when we'd have a home—a home that was ours, and that we'd never leave, and that we'd have for as long as God himself is with us, and that's forever, you know. Maybe it would be up in one of those stars, one of the bright ones, one of the bright stars, maybe the home would be there, I thought. And then I saw one, a real bright star, and I said that's it, that's maybe where we would all go, but not until it's the right time, not a second before, and I was glad then that we stayed around, and didn't all die, and I'm still glad.

"Oh, not all the time, I'm not all the time glad, I'll admit that. I was glad then, when my husband woke up, and he said he was sorry and he was glad, and he'd try to be good and not lose himself on account of wine. I was glad later, too. Most of the time I'm glad, actually. It's just sometimes I don't feel glad. I don't feel glad at all. Like my husband, I sometimes feel myself going to pieces; yes sir, that's how it feels, like you're going to pieces. Once I was real bad—real, real bad—and I thought I'd die because I was in such a bad way. I recall I'd have the same dream every single night, even every time I put my head down, it seeemd. It got so that I was scared to sleep, real scared. I'd try sitting up and resting, but not closing my eyes. After a while they'd close, though, and then it would come again, and the next thing I'd know I'd be waking up and shouting and crying and screaming, and sometimes I'd be standing up and I'd even be running around wherever we were staying, and my husband would be shaking at me, or my children, they'd be crying and telling me no, no, no it wasn't so and don't be scared, momma, and it'll be all right, they'd say. But I never believed them when I first woke up. It would take me an hour or so, I'd guess, to shake myself free of that dream, and I'd never really forget it, even when I'd be working. I'd be pulling the beans and putting them in the hamper, and I'd feel myself shaking, and there'd be someone nearby and she'd say, 'Martha, you took too much of that wine last night'; and I'd say no, I didn't touch a single drop, not last night or any other night for a long, long time. I wouldn't tell nobody, except my husband, but it was this dream I was having, and thank God now it's left me, but I can still see it, if I want to.

"There was a road, that's how the dream started, and it was all smoothed out and kept clean, and if you looked down on it you'd see yourself, like it was a mirror or something placed on the top of the road. I'd be standing there, and all of a sudden I'd see one car after the other coming, and inside the car would be one of my little ones, then there'd be the next child, and the next one, and each one had a car all to himself, and they'd be going down the road, almost as though they were going to go racing one another or something. But all of a sudden they'd explode, the cars would, one and then another, and soon they'd all be gone, and I couldn't find the sight of my children, and I'd still be standing there, where I was all the time, and I'd be shaking, whether in the dream or when I was waking up, I don't know. More than anything else, what hurt me was that the last thing that happened in the dream was that I'd see myself, standing on the road. I'd be looking down, and I could see my new child—yes, there'd be one I'd be carrying, and I'd be near the time to have the baby, and I'd be big and I'd be seeing myself, like in a mirror, like I said. But I'd have no other of my children left. They'd all be gone; and my husband, he'd be gone; and there'd be me, and my baby, not born yet, and that would be all. No, there'd be no cars, either. They'd all have gone and exploded, I guess."

How is such a dream to be analyzed or interpreted or made to explain something about her, about her wishes and fears and worries, about those things the rest of us would call her "psychological problems"? Why did the dream plague her then, seize control of her mind for those few weeks, then leave her, never to return? For all the world that separates her from me, for all her naivete (as it is put by people like me when we talk about certain other people) and my sophistication (as it is also put by people like me when we talk about ourselves) we could pursue the meaning of her dream without too much self-consciousness, and with a minimum of theoretical contrivance, density, or speculation. For several years, on and off, I had been telling her that I wanted to know how her children *felt,* how their spirits held up (or didn't) and she knew, right from the start, really, what I meant. In fact, once she told me what I meant: "I know. You want to see if they're scared, or if they're not. You want to see if they feel good, or if they feel lousy, real lousy, the way I guess their mother does a lot of the time!" So, the dream did not puzzle her all that much, only frighten her a lot, make her tremble, because at night she couldn't escape what by day she knew, could not help knowing— at every "level" of her mind, in her unconscious and in her subconscious and in her preconscious and in the thoroughly conscious part of her mind and yes, in her bones and her heart: "I'm always thinking, when I get ready to have another baby, that I wish I could be a better mother to them, and give them a better life to be born into than the one they're going to get on account of being my children, and not some other mother's. It's the worst of being a mother, knowing you can't offer your babies much, knowing there isn't much to offer them—there's really nothing, to be honest, but the little milk you have and the love you can give them, to start them off with. I know it's going to be bad for them when they grow up, and sometimes I wonder why God sends us here, all of us, if He knows how bad it's to be.

"There'll be a moment when I'll look at my children, and I'll wonder if they hold it against me for bringing them into this world, to live like we do, and not the others, with the money you know, and with the places where they can stay and not be always moving. The only rest we'll get, I'm afraid, the only rest we'll get is in the grave. Once, a long time ago, I said so, to my oldest boy, and he'll now and then repeat it to the younger ones. I want to tell him to stop, but I know he's right, and they don't get too upset with what he says, even if it's bad, like that. I think they sometimes don't really mind dying. God knows, they talk about it enough. Maybe it's what they hear from the minister. He's always telling us that everyone has to die, and that if you suffer here on earth you live longer in Heaven; and one of my girls, she said if that was the way, then maybe it was all right to be sick, but when you get to die, then is the time you're going to feel better, and not before then, no matter what you try to do."

Her children see no doctors for their various illnesses, and they don't actually "try to do" (as she put it) very much at all for themselves when they fall sick. They wait. They hope. Sometimes they say their prayers. Their mother also waits and hopes and prays, and apparently worries, too—and dreams and forgets her dreams and once, for a number of days, couldn't quite forget them, the terrible, terrible dreams that reflect in detail and in symbol the hard, hard life migrants live themselves, and see their children also as a matter of course begin to pursue. "I wouldn't mind it for myself," says the mother whose dream stayed with her so long, "but it's not good for the children, being 'on the road,' and when we're moving along I'll catch myself thinking I did wrong to bring all of them into the world—yes sir, I did wrong. But you can't think like that for too long, no sir, you can't; and I do believe the children, if they had their choice between not being born at all and being born and living with us—well, they'd choose to be themselves, to be with us, even if it's not easy for them and us, even so."

Sometimes when a mother like the one just quoted made an assertion like that to me, affirmed herself in spite of everything, said that there was after all a point to it all, a point to life, to life pure (and swift and unlucky) if not so simple, I felt in her the same questions I could not avoid asking myself. What *do* they think, those migrant children, about "life" and its hardships, about the reasons they must constantly travel, about the special future that more than likely faces them, in contrast to other American children? Does a migrant child of seven or eight blame his parents for the pain he continues to experience, day after day, and for the hunger? Does that child see his later life as very much like his father's or are there other alternatives and possibilities that occur to him as he goes about the business of getting bigger and working more and more in the fields? "What do *you* think?" I have heard from the mother who was once dream-possessed and from other mothers like her; and there does come a time when people like me ought to stop throwing questions like that back at the people who ask them (as if we have some royal privilege that grants us the right to do so) and spell out what, exactly, (if anything) we do think.

In my particular work, fortunately, the children—yes, uneducated migrant ones—have been quite willing to let me know what they see and think, what they believe about a number of matters. Like all children, they don't necessarily get into extended conversations; they don't say a lot, go into wordy descriptions of their moods and fantasies and desires and feelings. They do, however, throw out hints: they use their faces and their hands; they make gestures and grimaces; they speak out, with a phrase here and a series of sentences there. Moreover, it has

been my experience that they will also use crayons and paints to great advantage so that, given
enough time and trust, the observer (become
viewer) can see on paper, in outline and in
colors and shapes, all sorts of suggestive, provocative, and instructive things. When the
migrant child *then* is asked a question or two,
about this or that he has portrayed, pictured,
given form and made light or dark, there is,
I believe, a lot to be heard in those moments,
moments in a sense after the deed of creation
has been finished, moments when thoughts and,
more assertively, opinions can emerge from
something concrete, something done, even something achieved, in this case achieved by children
not always used to that kind of effort.

So, the children have drawn pictures, dozens
and dozens of pictures—particular migrant
children whom I came to know for two, maybe
three, sometimes four years, and whom at times
I asked to use paper and pencils and crayons
and paints in whatever way desired or for this
or that special purpose. I might, for instance,
want to see a favorite "spot" drawn, a place the
child especially liked, a house he might like, or
a camp he didn't like at all. I might want to

know about all those schools, about how they looked and how they seemed from the inside and how they can be compared, one to the other, the good and the bad, the pleasant and the very unpleasant. I might be interested in the crops, in which ones are good and bad to harvest, and how they look, the beans or the tomatoes or the celery or the cucumbers, when they are there, ready and waiting. I might ask about the essence of migratory life, about the way the road appears to the child, about what there is to be seen and noticed and sought out and avoided and enjoyed and shunned on those roads, about what remains in a given boy's mind or a girl's mind, when all the memories are sorted out, and one of them is left—to be chosen, to be drawn, and then reluctantly or shyly or cautiously or openly or even insistently handed to me as "it," as the thing done that was suggested or requested or hinted at or mentioned as a possible subject, one of many, but still one pointed out by me, and therefore to be done as a favor or in fear, or resisted out of the same fear (or anger) or absolutely refused, also out of fear or else confusion and often enough resentment.

What do they see, then—see in their mind's
eye, see casually or intensely—and through pictures enable others to see? Rather obviously,
many things are seen and even drawn or
painted; but there are, I believe, certain themes
that do come up repeatedly, no doubt because
migrant children share a number of habits
and concerns and cares and doubt. Tom, for
instance, was a seven-year-old boy when he drew
for me a rather formless and chaotic and dreary
picture (Figure 1) of the fields he already knew
as a helper to his parents, a harvester really,
because when he was five I saw him race along
those rows of beans—picking, picking, picking.
Once in a while he would show his age by shouting out his achievements, by pointing to anyone
near at hand how much he had just done, how
experienced he had become. Children we all
know are often like that, a little enthusiastic
and a little boastful. They will learn, we tell
ourselves, they will learn to take their own abili-
ties for granted, to deal less ostentatiously and
noisily with themselves and the world. I knew
Tom between the ages of five, when he started
working in the fields, and seven, when he still
worked at harvesting crops. I spent a lot of time
with him and his family during those two years

and since then have made a point of seeing him at least several times each year. (At this writing, he is no longer a child; he is fourteen and he lives with a woman and he is a father and like his parents he is a migrant farm worker—but that will have to be told elsewhere, when I describe the lives of grown-up, yes at fourteen, grown-up migrants.)

Tom always liked to draw pictures and in fact knew enough about what some people would call "the problems of representation" to appreciate his own failings: "I'm no good. I'll bet some kids can really do a good picture for you. Each time I try, but when it's done I can't say it looks the way I'd like it to look. It's not like it should be—real, I mean. I know you said it doesn't have to be, but is it a good picture if you have to tell someone what you've tried to draw?" I reassured him that time, and many other times. I gave him my prepared speech, full of encouragement and friendliness and praise, all of which, I have to add, I very much meant—because he did try hard, and his mind had a lot going on "inside" or "deep down," a lot that he very much wanted to put on paper and afterwards talk about.

He drew the fields, the dark, confusing, sun-

less fields—guarded, be it noted, by a black
fence and the outlines of some dark faceless
men. They were not in sight, those fields, because a strip of pines intervened—none of which
appears on the paper—but as Tom used his
crayons he could hear all sorts of sounds from
the migrants, who were eating their lunches
and talking and arguing and, in the case of
one man, singing. Tom worked on the grass,
used a wooden board I carried around, talked
as he drew, and interrupted his work to eat
his lunch. This is perhaps the point for me
to mention something about migrant children,
a "characteristic" I suppose it could be called:
in contrast to all other children I have observed
and worked with, migrant boys and girls are
quite willing to interrupt their particular tasks
—for instance, the doing of a picture or the
playing of various games with me—for any
number of reasons. It is not that they are agi-
tated or anxious or unable to concentrate and
finish what they start. It is not that they run
about helter-skelter because they are confused
or alarmed or afraid. It is not that they don't
understand what we are attempting and have
to move on rather than reveal their lack of com-

prehension. Some of them, like many other children, do have some of the difficulties I have just listed; but I emphatically do not have such essentially psychopathological matters in mind when I describe the apparent willingness of small children to take up a job, an assignment, a bit of labor, then leave what is being done for some other obligation or duty, which in turn is either finished or left half-finished so that the earlier task is once again taken up and in fact completed.

Here, I believe, one has to see the habits of children as vastly responsive to the habits of their parents. If parents take in their stride (because they have learned they must) the necessity for constantly moving from one field to another, from one responsibility to another, each of which can only be partially fulfilled by any given person and indeed requires a whole field of people, then it is only natural that the children of migrants will experience no great need to stay with things, to work at them endlessly and stubbornly or indeed consistently. Always, the child has learned, there is the next place, the next journey, the next occasion. The fields are there, being worked on when the child arrives with his parents. The fields are still there, and often enough are still being worked on when the child with his family leaves for another location, another cycle of arrival and initiative and involvement and exhaustion and departure—in the words of the Bible, words that in my opinion convey exactly what thousands of children feel, "world without end."

If Tom can distract himself for candy and coke yet return and finish what he has started, he can also do a quick turn of drawing or sketching and pause for discussion, which itself can be a pleasant distraction to a child not made anxious at the prospect of abandoning thoroughness for the sake of a whim, a change of direction or action: "I'd like to stop for a second, because when we're travelling on a road like that one, we'll have to stop, you know. My daddy, he says that a field isn't so bad when you're resting on it; it's only when you're picking that a field is so bad. No, most of the time we don't stop by the road. My daddy, he says you can get into a lot of trouble that way, because the police are always looking to see if we're not keeping moving, and if they catch you sitting by the road, they'll take you to jail and they won't let you out so easy, either. They'll make you promise to get away and never come back. They'll tell you that if you're going to be picking, you've got to go ahead and pick, and then you've got to get away, fast. That's why you have to watch where you're going when you're on the way to a farm, and you're not sure where it is. You've got to be careful, and the best thing is to follow someone who can lead you there, that's what my daddy says. Then, if you have to stop, you can find a path and go down it, and you'll be safe, and you won't end up being caught."

He does not seem to regard the fields as very safe or pleasant places to be. The more he works on his drawing of the fields, the more he seems compelled to talk about the subject: "I like to be moving along. If you keep moving you're safer than if you just stop in a field, and someone comes by, and they can ask you what you're doing, and they can tell you to get back in the car and go away as fast as the motor will go. Once I was really scared, and so was everyone else. We went way down a road that we thought was safe, and there was a little pond there, and we went and played in it, because

they said we could, momma and daddy did.
Then the man came; he was a foreman my
daddy told me afterwards. Then he said we
would all be arrested and we were no good, and
we should be in jail and stay there forever. My
daddy said we'd go right away, and we did, and
he said—the rest of the day he said it over and
over—that you're in trouble moving from one
state to the other, because the state police, they
don't like you, and the sheriffs, they don't like
you, and you know the foremen, they have
badges, and they can arrest you, and they have
men with guns and they'll come along and hold
one right to your ears and your head, and they'll
tell you that either you work or you move on up
the road, and if you sit there and try to eat
something, or like that, then you'll get yourself
in jail, and it won't be easy to get out, no sir.
That's why it's bad luck to stop and rest in a
field, and if you see one that has crops, then
it's bad luck, too—because you're lucky if you'll
have any money left, for all the work you do.
I don't like fields, that's what I think."

What else is there to say about Tom's drawing, about the fields in it, about the migrant life
he has already become part of? Tom looks upon

the fields and roads, the fields and roads that never really end for families like his, as both fearful and redemptive: "One thing I'll tell you, if it's real bad on a farm, if they're watching you too close and they don't pay you what they should, then you can sneak away in the middle of the night. Even if they have their guards looking over where you're staying, the guards will fall asleep and before they wake up, you can be on your way, and then you've got a chance to find a better place to work. That's why you have to keep your eye on the road, and when you leave it to stay in a cabin near a field, or in a tent like we were in the last time, then you should always remember the fastest way to the main road, and you should point the car so it's ready to go and all you have to do is get in the car and start the driving. It wasn't long ago that we did that, just packed up and left. We pretended we were asleep for a while, in case anyone was looking, and then in the middle of the night we up and went, and they probably didn't find out until it was morning, and by then we were a long way. And my daddy and the others, they checked in with this man they knew, and he gave them all work to do, picking beans, and he said he was glad to have them, and he'd give them every penny they earned, and not to worry. But my daddy says you never know if you should believe them or not, and a lot of the time they'll just double-cross you, and go back on their promise, and you're left with almost nothing, and there isn't much you can do, so you move on and hope it won't keep happening like that, no sir; and sometime it won't either, because you'll work, and then they'll pay you right what you deserve, and that makes it much better."

Does Tom wonder where it will all end, the travel and the new places to occupy for ever so short a time? Does he dream of some road that will lead to some other way of life? Does the continual motion make him grow weary and resentful, in spite of his own words to the contrary? Does he think about other children, who live not far from the roads he knows so well, children he occasionally, sporadically meets in a school where he attends classes for a month, or does he think of the school he liked but had to leave after two weeks? I have asked him questions like these, but I believe he answers them, in his own way, in many of the drawings he does, and often he condenses his answers in a particular drawing, such as the one in Figure 2: "I don't know where that road is going; I mean, no, I didn't have a road I was thinking of when I drew. I just made the road, and it probably keeps going until it hits the icebergs, I guess. I put some little roads in, but you shouldn't leave the road you're going on. I remember I asked my daddy once if he knew where the highway ends, the one we take North, and he said it probably ended where you get as far North as you can get—and there aren't any crops there, he said, so we'll never see the place, but it's very cold there, and maybe a lot of it has no people, because it's better to live where it's warmer. I said I'd like for us one time to keep going and see an iceberg and see what it's like there. My daddy said maybe we would, but he didn't mean it, I could tell. A lot of the time I'll ask him if we could go down a road further, and see some places, and he says yes, we can, but he doesn't want to. My momma says we've got to be careful and we can't keep asking to go here and there, because we're not supposed to and we'll get in trouble. She says we should close our eyes and imagine that there's a big fence on

each side of the road, and that we can't get off,
even if we wanted to and tried to, because of
the fence. That's why I put the fence in, a
little, to keep the car there from getting in
trouble with the police.

"No, I didn't mean for there to be a crash,
no. It would be bad if one happened. My
daddy's brothers, three of them got killed in a
crash. They were coming back to Florida from
up North, from New Jersey it was, and the bus,
it just hit a truck and a lot of people got killed.
They say the bus was old, and once down there
the brakes stopped working, but the crewleader
had it fixed, and it was supposed to be safe.
They were younger than my daddy, yes sir, and
he said he didn't see how it could be anything
but God's desire, that they should all, all of
them, be saved forever more from going up
and down through the states and never being
paid enough, except for some food and a place
to sleep, and after that, they don't give you
much money for anything else. I figured that
if I was picturing the road and me in the car,
I'd put a truck there, too; because, you know,
we see a lot of trucks and the busses, too, when

we go through Florida and then up North. But I hope the car and the bus in the picture don't crash like they do a lot of the time.

"Sometimes—yes, sometimes—I think to my-self when we're passing a town, that I'd like to look through the place and maybe stay there, I mean live there, and not go right on to the next place. I used to ask why, I'd ask my momma and my daddy and my uncles, but they all said I should stop with the questions, and stop trying to get a lot of reasons for things, and like that. In school once, in Florida it was, there was a real nice teacher (it was last year) and she said to the class that they should all be nice to me and the rest of us, because if people like us didn't go around doing the picking, then there'd be no food for everyone to eat, the fruit and vegetables. A girl laughed and said that was a big joke, because her daddy had a big farm, and he didn't use any people, just machines. I nearly asked her what her daddy was growing, but I didn't. I guess I was scared. The teacher didn't do anything. She just said we should go on and do our work, and the less trouble in the class the better it would be all the way around. I thought afterwards that I'd like to follow her home, the girl, and see if she was telling the truth; because I didn't believe her.

"I asked my daddy, and he said there are some farms like that, but not many in Florida, because the farmers need us to pick beans and tomatoes, and the machines cost a lot, and you can't get a second crop from the plants after the machine. No, I didn't speak to her, and I didn't follow her either. I mean, I did for a little while, but I got scared, and my friend, he said we'd better turn around or we'd be in jail, and we wouldn't get out of there for a long, long time. Then we did, we turned around, and when I told my sister (she's ten) she said we were lucky we're not there now, in jail, because the police, they keep their eyes on us all the time, if we leave the camps or the fields, to go shopping or to school or like that. I said one of these days I'd slip by. I'd get me a suit or something, and a real shiny pair of shoes, and I'd just walk down the street until I came to where they live, the kids that go to that school, and if someone came up to me and tried to stop me and if he asked me what I was doing, then I'd say I was just looking, and I thought I'd go get

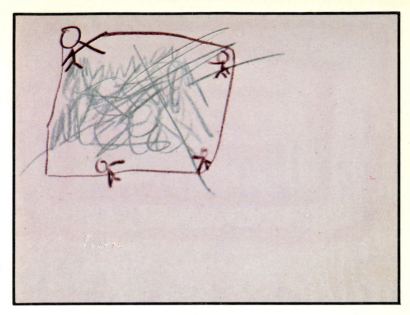

Figure 1

Figure 2

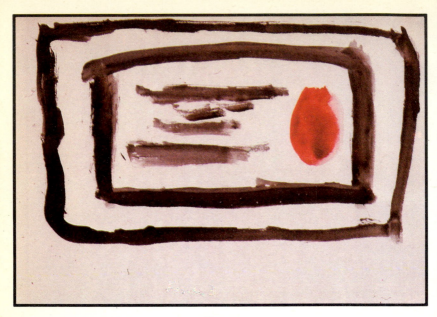

Figure 3

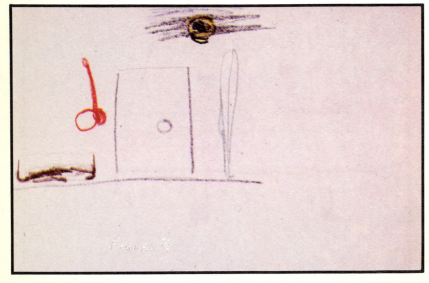

Figure 4

some ice cream, and I'd have the money and I'd show it to the policeman, and they couldn't say I was trying to steal something, or I was hiding from them, the policemen and like that. But my sister said they'd just laugh and pick me up, like I was a bean or a tomato, and the next thing I'd know I'd be there, in jail, and they might never let me out, except if one of the growers comes, and he would say it was okay if they let me out, and he'd pay the fine, but then I'd have to work for him.

"That's how you end up, I hear. They never do anything a lot of people, but work for the same man, because they always are owing him money, the grower, and he is always getting them out of jail, and then they owe him more money. My daddy says, and my sister, she says that the grower keeps on giving them the wine, and they drink it, and they'll be drunk, and the police will be called, and arrest them, and then the grower will come, one of his men mostly, and pay to get people out, and then they'll have to work some more—until they get killed. I hope it'll never happen like that to me. I'd like someday, I'll be honest, I'd like to go to the city, and I could get a job there. Once there was a

nice boy who sat beside me—not long ago, I
think it was this same year—and I was going to
ask him if I could get a job from his father.
No, I didn't want to ask him what his father's
job was, but he seemed like he was real rich, the
boy, and I thought maybe I could get a job, and
I could maybe live there, in the house there, you
know, where the boy does, and then I wouldn't
have to be going North later this year."

Would he miss his mother and father? "No—
I mean, yes. But I think they could come and
see me sometimes. If the people let me live in
their house, maybe they would let my daddy
come and see me, and my mother could come,
and they wouldn't stay too long, I know."

Migrant children see everything as temporary.
Places come and go, as do people, schools, and
fields. The children don't know what it is, in
Tom's words, to "stay too long"; rather, they
live in a world that lacks holidays and trips to
department stores and libraries. Children like
Tom, just quoted above, don't see any mail,
because their parents lack a home, a place from
which letters are sent and to which letters come.
Children like Tom don't know about book-
shelves and walls with pictures on them and

comfortable chairs in cozy living rooms and telephones (which are put by telephone companies into *residences*) and cabinets full of glassware or serving dishes or stacks of canned goods. Children like Tom don't even know about luggage; born to travel, born to live abroad the land, they nevertheless have to pick up and leave quickly, travel under constant surveillance, and never know quite what the next destination will bring in the way of work or living quarters, let alone pleasure. A suitcase hardly seems like a very important thing to any of us, yet migrant children have dreamed of having one, dreamed and dreamed and can say why after they draw a picture, as a girl of nine named Doris did: "I was smaller when I saw a store, and it had big suitcases and little ones; they all were made of leather, I think. I asked my mother if she could please, one day, get one for me, not a big one, because I know they must cost more money than we could ever have, but a small one. She said why did I want one, and I said it was because I could keep all my things together, and they'd never get lost, wherever we go. I have a few things that are mine—the comb, the rabbit's tail my daddy gave me before

he died, the lipstick and the fan, and like that
—and I don't want to go and lose them, and
I've already lost a lot of things. I had a luck
bracelet and I left it someplace, and I had a
scarf, a real pretty one, and it got lost, and a
mirror, too. That's why if I could have a place
to put my things, my special things, then I'd
have them and if we went all the way across the
country and back, I'd still have them, and I'd
keep them."

She still doesn't have her suitcase, the migrant
child Doris doesn't. In fact, Doris doesn't have
very much of anything, so that when I asked
her to draw whatever she wished, she answered
as follows: "I don't know if there's anything
I can draw." I suggested something from the
countryside. She seemed sad, after all, and in
no mood for my kind of clever silences, meant
to prod children like her into this or that psychological initiative (and revelation). She said
no, the countryside was the countryside, and she
sees quite enough of it, so there is no need to
give those trees and fields and roads any additional permanence. Rather, she said this: "I see
a lot of the trees and the farms. I'd like to draw
a picture I could like, and I could look at it, and

it would be nice to look at, and I could take it with me. But I don't know what to draw." Her judgement on the countryside was fairly clear and emphatic, but so was her sense of confusion. She knew what she didn't want to do, but she was at loose ends, too. She seemed to be asking herself some questions. What *do* I want to see, and carry with me through all those dismal trips and rides and detours and long, long, oh so long journeys? Where can I find a little beauty in the world, a touch of joy, a bit of refreshment and encouragement—and self-supplied at that, through crayons I have myself wielded on paper? Is there anything worth remembering, worth keeping, worth holding on to tenaciously, without any letup whatsoever? Perhaps I am forcing melodrama on Doris' mind, which certainly needs no more worries or fears. Perhaps for her life is a matter of getting up and working in the fields and eating what there is to eat and sleeping and moving on, moving here and there and always, always moving. I don't think so, though. For all the fancy words I use, and all the ambiguities and ironies I hunger after, the little girl Doris has insisted that I also listen to her. She has even made me realize I must do more than listen and observe and collect my "data" and, like her, move on: "If I draw a picture, a good one, I want to keep it. The last time you said you wanted it, and I told my mother I liked it and I wanted to keep it. I asked my mother if I could get some glue and put it on the window of the car, but she said no. She said we'd get stopped and arrested."

So Doris did two pictures at each sitting, one for herself and another one, as similar as possible, for me, all of which leads me to state another thing I have noticed especially among migrant children: unlike other children I have come to know, girls like Doris and boys like Tom don't want to give up drawings they make, not to me and not even to others in their family or to neighbors. In a world that constantly shifts (yet is the same) things like a drawing, worked on and made by the child himself or herself, can't be lightly dismissed, or even reluctantly dismissed. It is not a matter of property; nor does the child cling to the picture because he feels "realized" at last through something artistically done. Nor is he drawn irresistibly to the form and symmetry he has wrought, to all those colors at last made accessible to himself.

To be sure, it is all of that, which is a lot for young and impoverished wanderers. Doris one day told me why she wouldn't let go, and I fear I will have to let her explanation, unadorned by my translations and interpretations, stand as quite good enough: "I just want it—because it's good to look at, and it may not be as good as it could be, but it was the best I could do, and I can take it and look at it, and it will be along with me up North, and I can think of being back here where I drew it, and then I'll know we'll be coming back here where I drew it, and I can look ahead to that, you see." Doris did a second drawing, essentially the same, which she gave to me, then put the first version away, with her rabbit's tail and other belongings. She had done many other drawings for me, but somehow this one meant more to her than any of the others. It was as if she had finally found some kind of permanence for her meagre possessions, and also a talisman of sorts. So long as her things had a new and separate life of their own, in the picture, they would all be collected together, her little world of possessions, as they could not be in the suitcase that has never come. Now she could look ahead and look back and have some sense of direction, some idea of a destination, some feeling that life has its rhythms and sequences and purposes. But I said I would not do what I have just done, speak for her, be her interpreter.

We all are driven and compelled, whether we know it or not; the educated and well-analyzed are not the only ones who comprehend the mind's constraints. I have to make my little and not-so-little remarks, and Doris has to carry a few personal effects all over America. Another child known to me, whom I will call Larry, can spell out, can paint out if you will, the necessities that govern his particular life (Figure 3). What would he like to draw above all else, he was asked, and he said in reply that he didn't want to draw at all this time. He wanted to paint. Well, why did he want to paint this time? (Together, we had been using crayons for over a year.) "Oh, I don't know—except that tomorrow is my birthday." He was to be nine. Half because I wasn't actually sure what day tomorrow was, and half because, I suppose, I knew the *reason* why time had become blurred for me during the weeks I had moved about with Larry and his family, I asked him what day his birthday is: "It's in the middle of the summer, on the hottest day." He was dead serious, and I was both puzzled and embarrassed, a condition of my mind which he essentially noticed.

He was moved to explain things, to help me, to do what I am trained to do, formulate and soothe and heal. "I don't know the day. The teacher in one of the schools kept saying I had to bring in a certificate that said where I was born and gave the day and like that. I asked my mother and she said there wasn't any. I told the teacher, and she said that was bad, and to check again. I checked, and my mother said no, and so did my daddy, and so did the crewleader. He said I should tell the teacher to shut up, and if she didn't I could just walk out of school and they wouldn't go after me or give me any trouble at all. No, I didn't leave, no sir; I stayed there for as long as we did in the camp. It was the best school I'd ever seen. They had cold air all the time, no matter how hot it got. I wanted to stay there all night. They gave you good cookies all the time and milk, and the teacher, she said she wanted to buy us some clothes and pay for it herself. She said I should tell my mother to come to school and they would have a talk; and she said I should get my birth certificate and hold on to it. Then one day she brought in hers and showed it to us; and she said we all should stand up and say to the class where we were born and on what day of the year; but I didn't know. She said we should ask where our mothers were born and our fathers. So, I did and I told her I was born here in Florida, and my mother in Georgia and my father there, too; and my mother said it was a hot, hot day, and she thought it was right in the middle of summer, July it must be, she said, around about there, but she wasn't sure. Then I asked her if she'd go register me, like the teacher said, and she said I'd better stay home and help out with the picking, if I was going to go listening to everything and then getting the funny ideas and trying to get us all in trouble, because the crewman, he said if we started going over to the courthouse and asking one thing of them, and then another—well, they'd soon have us all in jail, my mother said."

He painted his certificate, and thus showed both me and himself that he could persist with an idea, an intention. Paint to him meant a more worthy and lasting commitment. To paint is to emphasize, to declare out loud and for all to hear, or so he feels: "If you paint a certificate it won't rub away, like with the crayons. I don't know how they make the real ones, but they have big black letters and one of them, it has a red circle—and the teacher, she said it was a *seal,* and it belonged to a city and it was put on a lot of important papers." If he had his certificate what would he do with it, once he had shown it to his teacher? He would keep it, treasure it, fasten it to himself in some foolproof way that he himself could only vaguely suggest rather than spell out: "I'd never lose it, like I did my belt. My daddy gave me a belt, and I was afraid if I put it on all the time, it wouldn't look so good after a while; so I kept it with me, and put it with my shoes and when we went to church I'd have on my shoes and my belt. But once in a camp there was a fire, and I lost my belt and my shoes; and I should have worn the belt, my mother said, or carried it with me wherever I went, even to the field. But I didn't, and too bad."

Shoes cannot be taken for granted by children like him, nor belts, nor socks, nor (so it seems) birth certificates, which presumably

everyone in America has. Since I know that children like Larry are born in cabins or even in
the fields, with no doctors around to help, and
since I know that they move all over and have no
official address, no place of residence, I should
not have been surprised that those same children lack birth certificates—yet I was. Sometimes we figure out the larger pattern of things,
do so coolly and systematically, and are brought
up short only by a minor detail here and there,
which suddenly makes us see a little more (yes,
that) but more significantly (and at last) begin
to feel—in this case, Larry's case—the rootlessness of a life, the catastrophic kind of empti-
ness he must live with all the time. Who am I?
Where do I come from? When did it really happen, my entrance into this world? Those are
questions which, after all, the rest of us never
stop asking, in one form or another; and they
are questions Larry asks himself in a specially
grim and stark fashion, because he really
doesn't have the usual, concrete answers, let
alone all the fancy, symbolic, or metaphysical
ones. Since he is, I believe, a bright and shrewd
child he won't quite let the matter drop, as
many migrant children at least seem to do. I'm

not at all convinced they actually do let what I can all too easily call "the matter" drop. Given a little acquaintance and the right conversational opening, I have heard other migrant children tell me what Larry has told me: it is hard to settle for near-answers and half-answers when the issue is *yourself,* your origins as a person and as a citizen.

Put a little differently, it is hard to be an exile, to be sent packing all the time, to be banished, to be turned out and shown the door. In the drawings of migrant children I constantly see, at no one's behest but their own, roads and fields (quite naturally) but also (and a little more significantly) those souvenirs and reminders of others places and times, when a comb was given as a present, when something that at least looked precious was found; and finally other drawings show even more mysterious objects, such as windows that are attached to no buildings and doors that likewise seem suspended in space. Why, exactly why, should a number of migrant children flex their artistic muscles over windows and doors, over sandboxes, or more literally, over a series of quadrangles? I cannot speak for all the migrant children I know, even as many of them cannot speak for themselves—only stumble upon their words, only stand mute, only look and grimace and smile and frown, only ask questions in reply to questions. Yet, a few of those children eventually and often unexpectedly have managed to have their say, managed to let me know what they're getting at and, by implication, what is preventing me from recognizing the obvious concerns of their lives. I have in mind a girl of eight who spends most of her time in Collier County, Florida and Palm Beach County, Florida, but manages a yearly trek north to upstate New York and New Jersey and into New England, into the farms of Connecticut. As I became a regular visitor of her family she, above all the other children, expressed an interest in the paints and crayons I brought along, as well as the various games. She loved a top I had, and a yo-yo. She loved the toy cars and trucks and tractors: "I know about all of those. I know my trucks. I know my tractors. I know the cars, and I've been in a lot of them." She once asked me how fast I've driven. She once asked me what it was like to be on an airplane. She once asked me if an airplane could just take off—and land on the moon or the stars or the sun. She once asked me why there are always clouds up North and why down South the sun is so mean and hot, so pitiless to people who don't own air conditioners or screens or even mosquito repellents or lotions to soothe burnt and blistered skin.

She was, in fact, always asking me questions and making sly, provocative, even enigmatic remarks. "I love the yo-yo," she told me, "because it keeps going, up and down, and that's what I do." What did she mean? "Well, we don't stay in one camp too long. When the crops are in, you have to move." As for the pictures she did, she liked to put a yo-yo or two in them ("for fun"), but most of all she liked to make sure the sun was blocked out by clouds that loomed large over the sketched or painted scene, which frequently would have a door or a window or both, along with a lone tree or some disorganized shrubbery. In one picture (Figure 4) she allowed a door to dominate the paper. I expected her to *do* something with the door, to attach it or use it in some way, but she simply let it be and went on to other things, to the sun and its grim face, to the clouds, those sad, inev-

itable clouds of hers, and to a sandbox and a
yo-yo, and, finally, to a tall plant which I
thought might be a small tree. I asked her about
that, the pine-tree, as I saw it. "No, no, it's a big,
tall corn. We pick a lot of corn up North." She
was, in other words, getting ready to go North.
It was early May, and soon they would all be
on the road. What does that mean, though, to
her—not to me, or to her parents, or to the
many, many teachers who see her so very briefly,
or to the crewleaders who will lead her family
on their annual journey? I've asked her that
question in various ways and she in her own
manner has replied—through her drawings and
paintings and in the games we've played and,
finally, with these words: "I hate to go, yes sir,
I do. I found some sand over there, and my
brother Billy and my brother Eddie and me, we
like to go and make things there. Soon we'll be
going, I know. I can tell when it's happening.
First we move our things into the car, and then
we go in, and then we go away, and I don't
know if we'll come back here or not. Maybe, my
mother says—all depending, you know. I try to
remember everything, so I won't leave anything
behind. Everytime we go, my daddy, he gets sore

at me, because at the last second I'll be running out of the car and checking on whether
I've left any of my things there. I'll go inside
and come out and then I know I haven't left
something."

Twice I watched her do just that, watched
her enter the cabin, look around and leave,
watched *her* watch—look and stare and most of
all touch, as if by putting her hands on walls
and floors and doors and windows she could
absorb them, keep them, make them more a part
of her. She is a touching girl. She touches. In a
minute or two, while the rest of her family
frets and adjusts themselves, one to the other
and all to the car which they more than fill up,
this little girl of theirs scurries about—inspect-
ing, scanning, brushing her body and especially
her hands and most especially her fingers on a
broken-down shack (no running water, no electricity) she is about to leave. When I saw her
look out of the window (no screens) and open
and close the door several times (it didn't quite
open or quite close) I realized at last what all
those windows and doors she drew might have
meant, and the sandboxes and the corn up
North, the corn that was waiting for her, sum-

moning her family, drawing them all from the cabins, making an uproar out of their lives: up and down, to and fro, in and out, here and there, they would go—hence the yo-yo and the windows from which one looks out to say good-bye and the doors which lead in and out, in and out, over and over again.

It is hard, very hard to take the lives of such children and do justice to them with words; and I say that because I have tried yet feel decidedly inadequate to the job. Of all the jobs I have had, to this one I feel particularly inadequate. I do not wish to deny these children, who like our own children are American citizens, the efforts they make every day—to live, to make sense of the world, to get along with one another and all sorts of grown-up people, to find a little pleasure and fun and laughs in a world that clearly has not seen fit to smile very generously upon them. Nor do I wish to deny these children their awful struggles, which in sum amount to a kind of continuing, indeed endless, chaos. It is all too easy, as I must keep on saying, for a doctor like me to do either—see only ruined lives or see only the courageous and the heroic in these children. I am tempted to do the former because for one thing there is a lot of misery to see, and for another I have been trained to look for that misery, see it, assess it, make a judgment about its extent and severity; and I want to do the latter as an act, perhaps, of reparation—because I have at times felt overwhelmed by the conditions I have witnessed during seven years of work with migrant farm families: social conditions, médical conditions, but above all a special and extraordinary kind of human condition, a fate really, and one that is remarkable and terrible and damaging, as I have said, almost beyond description.

In a way that has to be discussed, what Conrad called in *Heart of Darkness* "the horror, the horror" eventually has its effect on the observer as well as the observed, particularly when childen are the observed and one like me, an observer of children, does the observing. "The horror, the horror" refers to man's inhumanity to man, the brutality that civilized people somehow manage to allow in their midst. The crucial word is "somehow"; because in one way or another all of us, certainly including myself, have to live with, contend with even, the lives of migrant children—those I have just attempted to describe and hundreds of thousands of others—who live (it turns out, when we take the trouble to inquire) just about everywhere in the United States: North and South, East and West; in between; near towns or cities, and also far away from almost (but not quite) everyone's sight.

Somehow, then, we come to terms with them, who are, to take an expression literally and apply it very soberly, the wretched of the American earth. We do so each in his or her own way. We ignore them. We shun them. We claim ignorance of them. We declare ourselves helpless before their problems. We say they deserve what they get, or don't deserve better, or do deserve better if only they would go demand it. We say things are complicated, hard to change, stubbornly unyielding. We say progress is coming, has even come, will come in the future. We say (in a pinch) that yes, it *is* awful—but so have others found life: awful, mean, harsh, cruel, and a lot of other words. Finally, we say yes, it *is* awful—but so awful that those who live under such circumstances are redeemed, not later in Heaven, as many of them believe, but right here on this earth, where they become by virtue of extreme hardship and suffering a kind of elect: hard and tough and shrewd and canny and undeluded and undeceived and open and honest and decent and self-sacrificing and hauntingly, accusingly hard-working. I have at times, many times, done that, extolled these children and their brothers and sisters and cousins and friends and parents and grandparents and aunts and uncles; I have extolled them all almost to Heaven, where I suppose I also believe they will eventually and at last get their reward and where, by the way, they will be out of my way, out of my mind—which balks at saying what it nevertheless knows must be said about how utterly, perhaps unspeakably, devastating a migrant life can be for children.

I am talking about what I imagine can loosely be called psychological issues, but I do not mean to ignore the bodily ills of these children: the hunger and the chronic malnutrition that they learn to accept as unavoidable; the diseases that one by one crop up as the first ten years of life go by; diseases that go undiagnosed and untreated; diseases of the skin and the muscles and the bones and the vital organs; vitamin deficiency diseases and mineral deficiency diseases;

and untreated congenital diseases and infec-
tious diseases and parasitic diseases, and in the
words of one migrant mother, "all the sicknesses that ever was." She goes on: "I believe our
children get them, the sicknesses, and there isn't
anything for us to do but pray, because I've
never seen a doctor in my life, except once,
when he delivered my oldest girl; the rest, they
was just born, yes sir, and I was lucky to have
my sister near me, and that's the way, you
know." She has some idea about other things,
too. She thinks her children are living in hell,
literally that. She is a fierce, biblical woman
when she gets going—when, that is, she is talking about her children. I have heard the ser-
mons, many of them from her; and I see no
reason, after these years of work with mothers
like her and children like hers, to refuse her a
place in the last, sad summing up that merci-
fully allows an observer to pursue other matters
while the observed, in this instance, pursue all
they can possibly hope for, the barest, most
meager fragments of what can only ironically
be called *a life*.

"This life," says the mother, "it's no good on
me and my husband, but it's much worse than

no good on the children we have, much worse than it can be for any of God's children, that's what I believe. I'll ask myself a lot of the time why a child should be born, if this is the life for him; but you can't make it that we have no children, can you?—because it's the child that gives you the hope. I say to myself that maybe I can't get out of this, but if just one, just one and no more of my children·do, then I'd be happy and I'd die happy. Sometimes I dream of my girl or one of my boys, that they've left us and found a home, and it has a back yard, and we all are there and eating in the back yard, and no one could come along and tell us to get out, because we could tell *them* to get out, because it's our land, and we own it, and no one can shout at us and tell us to keep moving, keep moving. That's the life we live—moving and moving and moving. I asked the minister a little while ago; I asked him why do we have to always move and move, just to stay alive, and not have no money and die, and he said we're seeking God, maybe, and that's why we keep moving, because God, He travelled, you know, all over the Holy Land, and He kept on trying to convert people, to be good to Him, you know, but they weren't, oh no they weren't, and He was rebuked, and He was scorned (remember those words?) and He couldn't stay anyplace, because they were always after Him, always, and they didn't want Him here and they didn't want Him there, and all like that, and all during his life, until they punished Him so bad, so bad it was.

"The minister, he said if you suffer—well, you're God's people, and that's what it's about. I told him that once he preached to us and told us all morning that it was God who was supposed to suffer, and He did. Now it shouldn't be us who's going from place to place and, you know, nobody will let us stop and live with them, except if we go to those camps, and they'll take all your money away, that you must know, because they deduct for the food and the transporting, they tell you. Pretty soon they'll give you a slip of paper and it says you've worked and picked all the beans there are, and all the tomatoes, and the field is empty, and you've made your money, but you've been eating, and they took you up from Florida to where you are, and it cost them money to transport you, so it's all even, and they don't owe you and you don't owe them, except that you've got to get back, and that means you'll be working on the crops to get back South, and it never seems to stop, that's what. Like I said, should we be doing it, the crops all over, and without anything to have when it's over? They'll come and round you up and tell you it can be jail or the fields, that's what they will tell you, if you get a bad crewleader, that's what. Once we had a nice one, and he was always trying to help us, and he wanted us to make some money and save it, and one day we could stop picking and our children, they could just *be,* in one place they could be, and they wouldn't always be crying when we leave. But he died, the good crewman, and it's been bad since. You know, there comes a time, yes sir, there does, when the child, he'll stop crying, and then he doesn't care much, one way or the other. I guess he's figured out that we've got to go, and it's bad all the time, and there's no getting around it."

That is what the migrant child eventually learns about "life," and once learned finds hard to forget. He learns that each day brings toil for his parents, back-breaking toil: bending and stooping and reaching and carrying. He learns

that each day means a trip: to the fields and
back from the fields, to a new county or on to
another state, another region of the country.
He learns that each day means not aimlessness
and not purposeless motion, but compelled,
directed (some would even say *forced*) travel.
He learns, quite literally, that the wages of
work are more work, rather than what some of
us call "the accumulation of capital." He learns
that wherever he goes he is both wanted and
unwanted, and that, in any case, soon there will
be another place and another and another. I
must to some extent repeat and repeat the
essence of such migrancy (the wandering, the
disapproval and ostracism, the extreme and unyielding poverty) because children learn that
way, learn by repetition, learn by going through
something ten times and a hundred times and
a thousand times, until finally it is there, up in
their minds in the form of what I and my kind
call an "image," a "self-image," a *notion,* that
is, of life's hurts and life's drawbacks, of life's
calamities—which in this case are inescapable
and relentless and unremitting.

By the time migrant children are nine and
ten and eleven they have had their education,

learned their lessons. In many cases they have long since stopped even the pretense of school. They are working and helping out with younger children, or playing and getting ready for dating and loving, for becoming parents and following their parents' footsteps, thousands and thousands of those footsteps. As for their minds, they are, to my eye, an increasingly sad group of children. They have their fun, their outbursts of games and jokes and teasing and taunting and laughing; but they are for too long stretches of time downcast and tired and bored and indifferent and, to themselves, very unkind. They feel worthless, blamed, frowned upon, spoken ill of. Life itself, the world around them, even their own parents, everything that is, seems to brand them, stigmatize them, view them with disfavor, and in a million ways call them to account—lace into them, pick on them, tell them off, dress them down. The only answer to such a fate is sex, when it becomes possible, and drink, when it is available, and always the old, familiar answers: travel, work, rest when that can be had, and occasionally during the year a moment in church, where forgiveness can be asked, where the promise of salvation can be heard, where some wild, screaming, frantic, angry, frightened, nervous, half-mad cry for help can be put into words and songs and really given the body's expression—turns and twists and grimaces and arms raised and trunks bent and legs spread and pulled together and feet used to stamp and kick and move—always that, move.

"I do a lot of walking and my feet are always tired, but in church I can walk up and down, but not too far; and my feet feel better, you know. It's because God must be near." So she believes—that God is not far off. So her children believe, too. What is life like? One keeps on asking those children that question for the tenth or so time (or is it the hundredth time?) because—in their own manner—they do seem to want to talk about what is ahead for them; and *that,* one believes, is a good sign for them and a helpful thing (it must be acknowledged) for anyone who wants to find out about such matters, about what people see their life to be, their future to be—their destiny I suppose it could be called ordinarily—though whether migrants have any such thing is another matter.

"Well, I'll tell you," the girl says gravely in

answer to the question. Then she doesn't say anything for a long time, and the observer and listener gets nervous and starts rummaging for another question, another remark, to lighten the atmosphere, to keep things going, to prevent all that awkwardness, a sign no doubt of mistrust or suspicion or a poor "relationship." Yet, once in a while there does come an answer, in fits and starts, in poor language that has to be corrected a little later, but an answer it is—and a question, too, at the very beginning a question: "Well, I'll tell you, I don't know how it'll be ahead for me, but do you think my people, all of us here, will ever be able to stop and live like they do, the rest of the people?" No one knows the answer to that, one says, but hopefully such a day will come, and soon. "No, I don't think so. I think a lot of people, they don't want us to be with them, and all they want is for us to do their work, and then goodbye, they say, and don't come back until the next time, when there's more work and then we'll have you around to do it, and then goodbye again."

There is another pause, another flurry of remarks, then this: "I'd like to have a home, and children, maybe three or four, two boys and two girls. They could all be nice children, and they wouldn't get sick and die, not one. We would have a house and it would have all the things, television and good furniture, not secondhand. If we wanted to work the crops, we'd plant them for ourselves, because it would be ours, the house and the land we'd have and no one could come and take us away and take the house away, either. I'd make us all go to school, even me; because if you don't learn things, then you'll be easy to fool, and you'll never be able to hold on to anything, my daddy says. He says he tries, and he doesn't get tricked all the time, but a lot of the time he does, and he can't help it, and he's sorry we don't just stay in a place and he's sorry my sisters and brothers and me don't go to school until we're as smart as the crewmen and the foremen and the owners and the police and everyone. Then we could stop them from always pushing on us and not letting us do anything they don't want us to do. That's why, if I could, I'd like to be in school at the same time my kids would be there, and we'd be getting our education.

"I do believe we could have it better; because

if we could get a job in one of the towns, then we could get a house and keep it and not leave and then if I broke my arm, like I did, they would take care of it in the hospital and not send you from one to the other until you pass out because you're dizzy and the blood is all over, and it hurts and like that, yes sir. Also, we could go and buy things in the stores—if we had the money and if they knew you lived there and weren't just passing through. All the time they'll tell you that, they'll say that you're just passing through and not to bother people, and they don't want you to come in and mess things up. But I could have a baby carriage and take my babies to the shopping stores, like you see people do, and we could go into all of them and it would be fun. I'd like that. I'd love it. I'd love to go and shop and bring a lot of things home and they'd be mine and I could keep them and I could fix up the house and if I didn't like the way it looks I could change things and it would look different, and it would be better.

"My mother, she always says it don't make any difference how we live in a place, it don't, because we'll soon be leaving. If it's a real bad place, she'll say, 'Don't worry, because we'll soon be leaving,' and if it's a better one, then she'll say, 'Don't fuss around and try to get everything all fixed up, because we'll soon be leaving.' Once when I was real little, I remember, I asked her why we couldn't stop our leaving and stay where we are, and she slapped me and told me to stop bothering her; and my daddy said if I could find a better way to make some money, then he'd like to know it. But I don't know how he could do any better, and he's the hardest-working picker there is, the crewman told him, and we all heard. My daddy said if he would ever stop picking, he'd never, never miss doing it, but he can't, and maybe I'll never be able to, either. Maybe I'll just dream about a house and living in it. My mother says she dreams a lot about it, having a house, but she says it's only natural we would wish for things, even if you can't have them. But, if you're asking what it'll be like when I'm much older, then I can tell you it'll be just like now. Maybe it'll be much better for us, but I don't think so. I think maybe it won't be too different, because my daddy says if you're doing the work we do, they need you, and they're not going to let you go, and besides there isn't much else for us to do but what we're already doing. My brother, he thinks maybe he could learn to drive a tractor and he'd just go up and down the same fields and a few others, and he'd never have to go on the road like we do now; and he says when I think of going with a boy, I should ask him if he's going to go on the road, or if he's going to stay someplace, where he is, and get himself some kind of work that will let him settle down. But every time you try, they have no work but picking, they say, and the foremen, they're around, and soon the sheriff, and likely as not they'll arrest you for owing them something. If you get away, though, then you have to go someplace, and if you go to a city, then it's no good there, either, from what you hear, and you can't even work there, either; and it's real bad, the living, even if you don't have to be moving on up the road all the time.

"To me it would be the happiest day in the world if one day I woke up and I had a bed, and there was just me and a real nice man, my husband, there; and I could hear my children, and they would all be next door to us, in another room, all their own; and they would have a bed, each one of them would, and we would just be there, and people would come by and they'd say that's where they live, and that's where they'll always be, and they'll never be moving, no, and they won't have to, because they'll own the house, like the foremen do and the crewmen and everyone else does, except us. Then we won't be with the 'migrant people' anymore, and we'll be with everyone else, and it'll be real different."

So it would be, vastly different. She and children like her would see a different world. Unlike migrant children, other children like to draw pastoral landscapes, like to drench them in sun, fill them with flowers, render them anything but bleak. Unlike migrant children, other children don't draw roads that are fenced in and blocked off or lead nowhere and everywhere and never end. Unlike migrant children, most children don't worry about birth certificates, or doors and more doors and always doors—that belong, even in a few years of experience, to half a hundred or more houses. So again, it would be different if the little girl just quoted could have a solid, stable home. Her drawings would not be like the four I have selected, or like dozens of others very similar.

The themes would be different, because her life would be different. Her days and months and years would have a certain kind of continuity, a kind we don't think about because some things are so very important, so central to life's meaning and nature that we really cannot bear to think about them; and indeed if we *were* thinking about them we would for some reason have come upon serious trouble.

Even many animals define themselves by where they live, by the territory they possess or covet or choose to forsake in order to find new land, a new sense of control and self-sufficiency, a new dominion. It is utterly part of our nature to want roots, to need roots, to struggle for roots, for a sense of belonging, for some place that is recognized as *mine,* as *yours,* as *ours.* Nations, regions, states, counties, cities, towns— all of them have to do with politics and geography and history; but they are more than that, for they somehow reflect man's humanity, his need to stay someplace and live there and get to know—a lot, actually: other people, to varying extents, and what I suppose can be called a particular environment or space or neighborhood or world or set of circumstances. It is bad enough that thousands of us, thousands of American children, still go hungry and sick and are ignored and spurned—everyday and constantly and just about from birth to death. It is quite another thing, another order, as it were, of human degradation, that we also have thousands of boys and girls who live utterly uprooted lives, who wander the American earth, who enable us to eat by harvesting our crops— yes, as children they do—but who never, never think of any place as home, of themselves as anything but homeless. There are moments, and I believe this is one of them, when even doctors or social scientists or observers or whoever justly have to throw up their hands in heaviness of heart and dismay and disgust and say, in desperation: God save them, those children; and for allowing such a state of affairs to continue, God save us, too.

THE HORACE MANN LECTURE SERIES

1953 PUBLIC EDUCATION AND A PRODUCTIVE SOCIETY
Maurice J. Thomas

1954 THE SCHOOL THAT BUILT A NATION
Joy Elmer Morgan   (out of print)

1955 THE EDUCATION OF FREE MEN
Ernest O. Melby   (out of print)

1956 EDUCATION FACES NEW DEMANDS
Francis S. Chase

1957 FISCAL READINESS FOR THE STRESS OF CHANGE
Paul R. Mort   (out of print)

1958 FACTORS THAT INFLUENCE LEARNING
Daniel A. Prescott   (out of print)

1959 THE DISCIPLINE OF EDUCATION AND AMERICA'S FUTURE
Lawrence D. Haskew   (out of print)

1960 PSYCHOLOGY OF THE CHILD IN THE MIDDLE CLASS
Allison Davis

1961 PERSONNEL POLICIES FOR PUBLIC EDUCATION
Francis Keppel

1962 EDUCATION AND THE FOUNDATIONS OF HUMAN FREEDOM
George S. Counts

1963 A DESIGN FOR TEACHER EDUCATION
Paul H. Masoner

1964 CRITICAL ISSUES IN AMERICAN PUBLIC EDUCATION
John K. Norton

142